CW01522281

CRAZY LO

Crazy Love: fifty therapy lessons

Published by Adam Rei Books in 2020

A first edition of this book was published
by Irene Press in 2015 under the title
Love & Sex: fifty therapy lessons

Copyright © Patricia Morris 2015; 2020.

ISBN: 978-1-911047-54-4

All rights reserved. No part of this publication may be used or
reproduced, stored in a retrieval system or transmitted in any form -
electronic, mechanical, photocopying, recording or other - without the
prior permission in writing of the copyright owner.
300920-202-30248

Cover design: Print Tailors
www.printtailors.com

Also by this author
Freud, Politics and Civilisation: an essay
Fetishism, Psychoanalysis, Anthropology
Albert Schweitzer: the Difficulty of Doing Good
Albert Schweitzer: Cold War Casualty

CRAZY LOVE:
fifty therapy lessons

PATRICIA MORRIS

CONTENTS

1
Introduction

This is not a book for romantics or starry-eyed optimists. It is for pragmatists interested in the process of psychotherapy and counselling and for those who want to explore various means to diminish the emotional pain that attaches to sensations of love.

The book covers fifty associated topics, material that frequently arises in psychotherapy or counselling sessions about love and sexual relationships. These are lessons learnt over many years spent listening to patients.

The sections can be read in any order but since the first ten sections focus on the process of counselling and psychotherapy, the reader interested in the profession may find it useful to start at the beginning.

A psychotherapist's job is to listen with a particular kind of attention to patients trying to speak about what is difficult to speak about, their darkest, most distressing, secret selves. Contrary to the caricature of the occupation as catering to a middle-class indulgence, the psychotherapist must be made of the strongest stuff in order to manage properly and professionally the Pandora's box opened by people from all walks of life. Of course, this includes the middle-classes. Their psychological histories, it turns out, are as fraught as anyone's.

It is hardly surprising that *bona fide* training to become a psychotherapist is demanding and long. The strictures for confidentiality are severe. Partly for this reason, ironically, misconceptions about the profession and its patients persist.

Where the discussion that follows gives clinical examples, patients' permissions have been obtained to use certain material even while all identities have been concealed and circumstances have been altered to avoid any chance of recognition. Nevertheless, the point of the exercise is lost if readers don't frequently encounter uncannily familiar patterns of behaviour or vivid aspects of themselves or people they know. As unique as we each are, it is astonishing how much alike we can make ourselves. This book is an attempt to capture that.

***

Psychotherapy methods: There are many therapy methods, each with its own terminology. For the sake of simplicity here, the terms therapist, psychotherapist, counsellor and psychoanalyst are often conflated. The methods of practice drawn upon here are the ones that adopt a conventional moral compass, that respect confidentiality, that keep clear physical, social and professional boundaries between practitioner and patient, and that assume the relevance, though not always the supremacy, of psychoanalytic concepts such as the unconscious, transference and counter-transference.

Adults and children: While the focus is on adults not children, it is never far from view that we ourselves have all been children. Our early experience of our parents or parent surrogates, in both obvious and insidious ways, continues to be

3

the primary influence in shaping our adult lives. The child in each of us is still always making its presence felt.

Gender: Given our hyper-sensitivity to social and political equality in the last fifty years, feminists in particular will be struck by how deep are the emotional and psychological differences between what we may summarise as being the male and female positions. Sadly, for all that has been achieved, in our interactions with the world exterior to our psyches, we are still far away from the broad ideals of what used to be thought of as women's liberation. Despite our new cultural achievements, and although we baulk at admitting it, women often covertly or unconsciously submit to the male position, to men.

When viewed through the psychoanalytic lens, there is an arbitrariness to sexual difference. The roles of the male or female partners in a couple are reversible and interchangeable, occasionally indistinguishable. The masculine position can as well be occupied by a biological woman and the feminine position can as well be occupied by a biological man. These apparent reversals do not necessarily imply an effeminate man or a masculine woman and besides, while the emphasis varies, in each of us there is a constant movement to and fro between these positions.

The examples cited in this book often but not always use the artificial convention of the female therapist and the male patient discussing a heterosexual partnership. This is merely a technical conceit in order more easily to distinguish between two parties in a textual description. Usually it works, sometimes it sounds clumsy, always it is annoying, not least when the individual you're identifying with in the argument is not of your gender. There is no easy way to navigate these changeable currents.

2
Advice about advice

The psychotherapist's opening gambit in a first therapy session is often to the effect: "Don't expect me to give you advice. The therapist's role is at the most to help you find your own way."

Beware of generalisations and beware of certainties, not least those contained here. Most of them won't hold true in all possible circumstances. In real life everything is always more complicated.

3

How psychotherapy works or doesn't

Psychotherapists strive to maintain a particular kind of attentive stance while listening to the patient speak, neither judging the patient nor presuming to know quick solutions for his or her problem.

The patient is encouraged by the psychotherapist to practise being ruthlessly honest in therapy sessions, to observe and describe any signs of suppressing particular thoughts and feelings or disguising them as others. Of course, it is impossible to eliminate self-deceit, to have only a single facet to one's being.

An aim of therapy is to make time to speak so that one can think anew and speak differently about oneself in a safe context. Freud discovered that "free association", the difficult task of speaking without self-censorship, is the best way to produce glimpses of disguised or hidden thoughts and feelings. Only once unconscious information becomes conscious can it be addressed.

The insight that accompanies bringing unconscious material to consciousness has a cathartic effect. Freud's intention was that he and the patient then apply conscious cerebration in order to make sense of previously obscured material.

The benefit of the psychoanalytic method is not only in the patient's free association in his speech – although this may indeed allow for some venting of emotion. This is merely the catalyst and conduit for the production of material preliminary to the work of interpretation of what the patient says.

An interpretation may be evident immediately or may require further associations of ideas that take many sessions to emerge. Interpretation does not so much lead to an ultimate answer as to receptivity to a useful question.

When you hear that someone has stopped

going to therapy "because the therapist never says anything" it could well be that the therapist has simply not yet found a productive balance between, on the one hand, allowing the patient time and space for his cathartic explorations and on the other hand, threading together the interpreted material so that the patient can contemplate it consciously.

The process is slow and delicate and is easy neither for the therapist nor the patient. The complexity of the human psyche forbids isolating finite solutions to all problems.

When therapy fails — which usually means that the patient stops coming to sessions — it is possible that it has little to do with the therapist's deficient skill or method and everything to do with the patient's impatient need for an — unrealistic — quick fix; or it may have to do with his resistance to self-exploration. Unravelling the knots of a patient's resistance is one way of summarising much of the therapy process.

The least a patient can hope for in going into psychotherapy is to have a safe place to speak of what he hardly knows he wants to say. Talking to a non-judgemental professional practitioner can help one articulate and disentangle difficulties so that they can be diminished, dissolved, or escaped.

4

Resistance or addiction to psychotherapy

It requires a trained and experienced therapist to arouse the patient's curiosity about himself and to keep him coming back to sessions despite his reluctance to enter the emotional territory that he has always needed to ignore.

Psychotherapy initially can be a little disconcerting for some patients because it uncovers new ideas and emotions that they may have spent a lifetime consciously or unconsciously avoiding. Then again, sometimes this is exactly the reason that the patient wants to have therapy. He is ready to face something about himself that hitherto he has fled. He senses that the therapist's neutral, professional distance from him can provide support through a period that may be testing. Entering this territory with someone close to him, a friend or family member, would be less productive and more uncomfortable for him.

A patient can become anxious before he becomes curious. He may find excuses to miss sessions or to turn up late or on the wrong day. He may stop attending sessions altogether. He may use the convenient excuse that "nothing happens" in a therapy session and "there's no sign of progress" between sessions or, conversely, that the sessions make him "think too much". He blames his bad moods on events that are happening around him rather than inside him. For a short time, unhappiness that he has suppressed may well up volubly with his family and friends. They may attribute his unsettled conduct to the therapy or the therapist. They may advise him to stop seeing her.

Often a patient decides not to return to therapy just when useful therapeutic work is starting to happen. The pattern of resistance and flight from help can show itself in any patient, in people with afflictions as diverse as anxiety, depression, phobias, obsessions, addictions, eating disorders, and a lot else. Perhaps the patient can't bear the imminent possibility of confronting, say, his sadness, or his wounding of himself or of others. The therapist will take a view as to whether the patient should struggle on or abandon the therapy work. It's usually the former and the therapist will calibrate her approach according to the response of the patient.

Our barely conscious anxiety makes it difficult to find a reasonable, balanced route through life, a route that is a safe distance from, say, inertia or manic consumption or rage on the one side and varieties of questionable self-denial on the other. Serious addicts, that is, those unfortunates whose daily equilibrium has been trashed by their addiction, will defend against having to give up entirely their preferred opiate, whether it be bullying or apathy or sex binges or over-eating or drugs or alcohol or gambling or rages or self-loathing — or mere self-righteousness.

When a patient becomes keen on attending regular therapy sessions, there are invariably a few people, not himself, who call it an addiction. If psychotherapy is conducted properly, it is too transparent an exercise to become an addiction for the simple reason that the process of therapy explicitly interrogates itself. Its only secrets are those that the patient wants to keep from himself.

5
Psychotherapy's customs and terminology

Psychotherapists and counsellors treat people wanting to find it in themselves to alleviate or manage their distress. Most therapists elect to train to practise the method of one particular school of thought and believe that theirs is the best method.

To summarise the difference between psychotherapeutic methods one needs to make an artificial and admittedly simplistic distinction between three groups of trained practitioners in the field. Let us say that the first group is that of the *psychoanalytic psychotherapist* and the *psychoanalytic counsellor*, the second that of the *classical psychoanalyst*, and the third that of a vast and ever-increasing population of practitioners in a burgeoning industry of methods ranging from cognitive-based to spiritual, including "alternative" and "humanist" therapists.

During a session some therapists in the third group, just for example, may hold hands with or even hug a patient to demonstrate sympathy. In sharp contrast, bodily contact with a patient is anathema to the work of psychoanalytic practitioners. This book does not deal with practitioners in the third group but it is useful to have some idea of its broad characteristics.

In the methods that concern us here, therapists avoid physical contact wherever possible, some, such as myself, preferring not even a handshake of greeting or farewell.

We should note that outside Britain and parts of Europe the term "psychoanalyst" or "analyst" is used loosely, often instead of the term psychotherapist. This partly accounts for people's confusion regarding the meaning of these terms. A *psychiatrist* is a medical doctor who has specialised in medical aspects of the brain, the mind and the body. A *psychologist,* a member of the broadest sub-category in our general category, is someone who has studied the relationship between the mind, emotion and behaviour. Psychologists will each specialise in a sub-set of a large array of possibilities, such as child development or forensics or disability or learning or language or animal behaviour and so on.

According to the British Psychoanalytical Society (BPAS), anyone who has not completed its unique training at the Institute of Psychoanalysis in London and who labels himself or herself a "psychoanalyst" is falsely claiming to be a qualified member of the BPAS. By this measure there are few authentically trained classical psychoanalysts in the world. That said, there is an audible lobby within the BPAS recognising that in fact each psychoanalyst's practice is so varied in its arrangements with patients that the term psychoanalytic psychotherapist, which will be discussed below, can as well be applied accurately to most psychoanalysts.

You can recognise a classical psychoanalyst's initial self-presentation to the patient because she will tend to be silent and formal, attempting to erase any display of her personality and individuality. A patient can experience this reserve as coldness or rudeness or shyness or social ineptitude. It is impossible to say whether he is accurately seeing through the analyst or whether he is misunderstanding her intention because methodologically she is obliged to present a blank screen rather than make a show, for instance, of conviviality.

Almost always in classical psychoanalysis, and sometimes in psychoanalytic psychotherapy, the patient lies on a couch and the analyst sits behind the head of the couch so that there is no eye contact between them during the course of the session. The interactions between patient and analyst (or therapist) have a distinctly different quality when there is no eye contact.

The use of the couch facilitates but is not essential to the production of what is termed the "transference". The so-called transference is, crudely put, the patient's unconscious relationship with the person whom he at any moment supposes the analyst to be.

All practitioners observe professional boundaries of conduct. They are cautious about disclosing personal information partly for ethical reasons but also because obviously the act of divulging personal information complicates the transference.

The "therapeutic alliance" and the complex "rapport" between the patient and therapist are important in the psychotherapeutic process. They are set up variously according to the therapist's mode of training. A patient's transference in the session is distinct from his rapport with the therapist. Good rapport in the therapeutic relationship, which is critical to the work, is not, one must stress, synonymous with a happy, friendly atmosphere. Good rapport is perfectly compatible with the patient's resistant, depressed, anxious or even adversarial stance in the session. Good rapport has something to do with the patient's sense of trust and safety, or, if that is fragile, the patient's openness to the therapist's skill at working with the patient's lack of them.

The difficulties that the patient throws across his own path on the way to accessing information about himself may be summarised by the term "resistance". Analysing the patient's resistance is an important part of all psychotherapy.

A classical psychoanalyst sees her patient for three, four or five sessions a week. If the sessions are less frequent then the process is not strictly speaking psychoanalysis but, rather, psychoanalytic psychotherapy. It must be stressed again that the divisions being made here between therapeutic practices are formulaic. In reality, a classical psychoanalyst may be able to see a patient only once a week and a psychotherapist's patient may use the couch three times a week.

The patient who elsewhere feels unheard, unseen or not listened to, may find his suffering at last dignified by the serious attention given it by the analyst or therapist. The patient now has a regular, unique period of time to speak and listen to himself in a safe setting as a means to his finding his own way to think differently, perhaps with the help of the therapist's measured, even tentative interpretations of the transference or his resistance.

*

Remarkably often in the cinema, the director of a scene with an actor-patient on the couch in a session with his actor-analyst will position them so that they can see each other's facial expressions. This is a curious and mistaken cinematic custom. It is a convention akin to that of the actor-driver, with whom we are all familiar, who barely watches the road as he chats to his passenger, or the actor-painter at his easel who holds the paintbrush as if it were a pen, or the actor-aristocrat dining grandly and waving his cutlery about as he pontificates. It is a film, it doesn't matter, but it's worth bearing in mind that a movie depicting a therapist and patient is not a reliable source of information about what actually goes on in a session — probably because what actually goes on has almost no cinematic value.

6

Psychotherapy's boundaries and transgressions

It is the psychotherapist's responsibility to care for the fragile and therefore suggestible aspects of the patient's psyche, not to exploit or abuse them.

Whatever the counsellor or psychotherapist's manner, whether it is formal and silent or relaxed and apparently friendly, you may be sure that she is carefully calibrating and managing the interaction with her patient. Theirs is not a social encounter. The therapist's firmly held professional stance, which need not be an imitation of an iceberg, is a prerequisite in a therapy session.

Similarly, it is impossible for a therapist to conduct an authentic therapy session with a close friend or family member, or for that matter with the stranger seated beside her at a dinner party.

Psychotherapy depends for its efficacy on a skilfully managed interchange across a carefully maintained therapeutic distance separating the therapist from the patient. Their interchange occurs at the intersection between the patient's spontaneous speech to an unknown "Other" and the therapist's ability to interpret the patient's words constructively and confidentially.

The classical psychoanalyst is able to make hair-splitting choices about when to speak and what to say to a patient during a session. The rarity of her speech may result in the patient attributing monumental importance to her every word. It is not unusual for a patient to ponder and fret for days over an analyst's choice of preposition or her timing of a response.

This happens too with the patients of a psychotherapist or counsellor but the effect of her speech may be less weighty because it's more likely that the patient's interrogation of it will not always be met with silence or a reflecting question. Although the counsellor or psychotherapist may allow for more verbal interaction in the therapy room, all psychoanalytically inclined practitioners are always working hard, even, or especially, when silent.

More than once I have been told of a psychoanalyst falling asleep during a patient's session when the patient was on the couch. Psychoanalyst Anna Freud famously knitted while conducting sessions. A venerable, respected and busy senior psychoanalyst told me that throughout her own career, which spanned the second half of the last century, when a patient was on the couch she had embroidered tapestries because she hadn't wanted to "waste time". She said that it hadn't interfered at all with her attentiveness to the patient's words and that it was not unusual for psychoanalysts of her generation to engage in sewing, darning, crocheting and knitting while the patient lay on the couch. Such activities, as well as falling asleep, would be impossible for a present-day counsellor or psychotherapist. Face to face therapy today requires intense concentration and a quality of speech engagement with the patient that precludes other activities — including nodding off.

Therapists are ethically bound by their

trainings' rules to prioritise their care of the patient's vulnerability in a session. Serious aberrations of a therapist's conduct are extremely rare, almost unheard of, despite what the press and popular movies would have one think. A patient's discomfort in a session is more likely to be occasioned not by the therapist but by the patient being unable to cope with hearing what he wants to say about himself. Nevertheless, if a patient feels that the therapist is acting or speaking in a way that transgresses a professional boundary, he should not hesitate to question or even stop the proceedings and then, if possible, to discuss the matter with the person who was the source of the referral.

A patient's distress may be caused by experiences that to an outsider could appear slight but which to the patient are nothing of the sort: he has unconsciously pathologised them according to his own emotional lesions. For one patient, revealing, say, his religion or the nationality of a parent or his sexual preference may feel deeply self-exposing to him. For another patient, those matters are trivial compared to admitting to being haunted by, say, a legal or moral calamity in his family's distant history. The subject matter that perturbs individuals varies greatly and the therapist tries to learn over time to pick her way carefully with each patient to discover whether a topic creates apparent awkwardness attributable to quantifiable cultural norms or to deep and idiosyncratic psychological factors.

It sometimes occurs that a patient develops strong positive feelings for the therapist and after struggling to keep silent about the matter, confesses, as it were, to the therapist. At such periods the therapist always maintains the professional, non-judgemental boundary with the patient. Useful therapy work can be done in discussing the patient's transference, that is, his emotions and suppositions about the therapist and other objects of desire.

If you ever hear of a therapist who has ended up in a reciprocated romantic relationship with a patient, you may be sure that whatever was going on in the sessions beforehand, it wasn't therapy. Nor was it the patient's fault or responsibility to see that the "romance" didn't happen. If a therapist is doing his or her job properly, it is impossible for either of them to form an ordinary social relationship that can lead to physical or emotional intimacy.

Love and sexual attraction, as much of this book demonstrates, require a cumulative, knowing surrender of one's rational faculties to the service of the libido. This process entirely contradicts the vigilant quality of interaction that from the start is established and managed by a professional therapist with his or her patient in order to conduct constructive psychotherapy or counselling sessions.

Portia

I heard once of a young woman, let's call her Portia, whose doctor had referred her to a counsellor who was starting part-time work in the small town where she lived. A few nights after their first session the "counsellor" phoned Portia to say that he'd been reviewing his notes and would she please describe to him more fully the sexual dreams she had referred to during their counselling session. She thought this was a strange request. She replied that she would rather wait to tell him at their next session. After his phone-call she began to fret about whether she was being unduly suspicious of him but she felt that if her suspicion was justified, it could be hazardous to have further sessions with him. Because she was in a fragile state anyway, and because she had faith in the referring doctor's good intentions, and because she had no previous experience of what usually might be discussed in — or out of — a counselling session, Portia wasn't able to trust her own sagacity about the ethics of the counsellor's conduct. Fortunately, she had the good sense to tell a friend about the counsellor's unexpected phone-call. The friend put her in touch with her own therapist who advised Portia to discontinue sessions with that particular counsellor and to inform her doctor about what had happened so that the matter could be formally dealt with. Fortunately, experiences such as Portia's are very unusual.

7

The reluctant patient

Amongst those who attend a therapy session, while some may be fearfully ambivalent about taking the risk of exploring aspects of themselves in order to come upon what is hidden there, one can't ignore the fact that they have indeed attended a session. This suggests curiosity and courage, that is, underlying psychological health.

A patient's refusal to speak openly can happen even when the setting is entirely safe, when the therapist has ample social and professional skills, when the patient trusts that no harm can come to him by talking. Such a patient may still be locked in by fear, stuck in a state of passivity. For the present, he desires action – someone else's action. He wants work to be done, hard work, but not his own work. "You're being paid to fix me, so fix me," might be his unspoken, or even spoken, script. He wants answers without his doing the personal archeology that will uncover the question.

Aside from his fear, this attitude implies a commonly held mechanical view of the human psyche, a belief that people operate in much the same way as machines: an expert inserts a batch of data on one side and a predictable and improved result pops out on the other.

Reluctant patients at some time in their past unwittingly may have been trained to hide their vulnerability but they know that all is not as they wish it to be. They're cautious about entering their interior world in case they have to own up to a certain part of themselves, or of those close to them, that they would rather deny is there. Psychotherapy aims to assist someone in talking about these difficult reaches of the psyche so that the sense of, say, fear or shame or disgust or rage that the patient attaches to them can be dismantled in a safe, non-judgemental place.

Showing one's vulnerability is a precondition for therapy to occur but is not, as in confession, an end in itself. Only by trying to get behind one's mask of ignorance and pretence can one begin a tolerant and cognitive acquaintance with the feelings concealed there.

The process is slow, not least because often a typical first move is for the patient to hide behind a screen of apparent confession. Perhaps he habitually reveals a measure of vulnerability that belongs to a manageable area of his life on which he can knowingly expend self-deprecating humour. The best stand-up comedians, for instance, famously exploit their special gift for this. Most of us are adept at distracting an interlocutor from our subterranean truths. It is an automatic survival mechanism that works well — until it doesn't.

Helena

Here's an example. After some two years of therapy a patient, let's call her Helena, found that her self-esteem had increased. She worked at the cutting edge of the music industry, a notoriously difficult arena in which to remain on an even keel. She said that everything would have been different had she recognised when she was much younger how submissive and gullible she had always been. Now instead of being crushed by her meekness, she was always angry with the younger self she had once been.

Before she went into therapy she'd been at the mercy of a life-long persona, that of "the only child" of an uninterested, single, busy mother. At school she had been desperate for any companionship and found herself being manipulated by the cool, critical crowd with whom she fell in. At first they had made her their little mascot and then in the guise of daring her to take even more chances than they themselves took, had consistently bullied her, trashing any last vestige of her self-confidence.

With therapy she became braver about asserting herself when parents or friends or work-colleagues attempted to boss her around. She stopped binge-drinking at club-nights. She stopped being promiscuous, a kind of conforming behaviour that she had repeated for years in order to do as the others did.

Eventually Helena simply stopped seeing her circle of competitive so-called friends. Her social life shrank but she didn't care now. She revelled in being more in charge of herself, in her corresponding success in the work-place, in having more interesting friends. Once she had broken the pattern, she found that she didn't miss the hangovers or the amnesiac one-night-stands. She didn't miss the compulsion to keep trying to belong to a crowd that she didn't even like. She was proud that she had cleared away the danger-strewn miasma in which she formerly had wandered thoughtlessly and self-destructively.

These were substantial changes for a person to have made in a relatively short time. For several months Helena repeated the plaintive or angry refrain that she wished she'd started therapy years before.

Significantly, with all her hopeful and regretful realisations, she began to find it impossible to come to therapy on the same weekly basis. Money was not the issue as by now her standard of work had escalated and with it her salary level. Even when she could have had video therapy sessions to accommodate her travelling schedule, even though her frequent cancellations and excuses were often legitimate, it was obvious that she was slowing down the therapy but not feeling able to end it.

Helena had persuaded herself that she was a "therapy success story". True, she had vanquished so many of her material and emotional addictions, and what's more, had ascended the work ladder. Now, she said, she needed a counselling session for "a fix" only when she was hit by a mini-crisis. She wanted the comfort of knowing that rescue was easily at hand when and if she called for it, rescue in the form of her therapist as the benign surrogate mother.

She had given up a lot of her self-destructive patterns but she couldn't bring herself to surrender to the discipline of scheduling a regular time to reflect anew on herself. What was different? For all the indubitable gains in her more mature self-image, her achievements highlighted the contrast with what she felt she had always lacked and still lacked.

Continuing regular therapy was not so appealing when the next phase would mean considering the fallout from exchanging party-girl excess for career-woman success. She might have to re-visit unhappy early memories of having been an ignored, little loved, lonely only child. If she stopped the therapy, the memories could be blocked out by her busy and productive work schedule. The memories haunted her when she took a break, when she was on her own. Then she would be struck down with bouts of distress at neither having a man in her life nor being a mother: not being the woman her own mother had not been.

Helena was as yet unable to find the courage to enter the next productive phase of therapy yet her reluctance to end the therapy completely, her insisting on an occasional session, keeping a thread of connection — calling it "a fix" — suggested that when she found the emotional wherewithal, she would resume the therapy.

8

When one partner wants the other partner in therapy

The aggrieved partner in a sexual relationship sometimes believes that psychotherapy, or a psychotherapist, will go to work on the wrong-doer's mind, or perhaps brain, and transmogrify it into what the unsatisfied partner wants it to be. He or she supposes that the therapist's expertise will bring the errant wanderer's hurtful capers or depressive withdrawal or angry criticisms into alignment with the "normal" conduct that anyone — meaning the complaining partner — might expect.

This kind of wishful thinking is surprisingly common.

People change in the course of a psychotherapy but the direction of the change can hardly be predicted. There is no knowing in advance of the process whether the philanderer or the chronically ill couch-potato or the tantrum-thrower will discover that his unfaithfulness or his inertia or his rage has obscured anxieties that can be dealt with by or after improving the relationship in the course of having psychotherapy. Perhaps, rather, in therapy he will discover that he's simply not cut out for the relationship at all. The partner who forces him to get therapy may get much more than was bargained for. Or much less.

Therapy's aim is not to readjust the patient's relationship to suit the wishes of one half of the couple. It has only an approximate aim and it is rather modest: that the patient become able to think differently and therefore eventually lead a less troubled life.

9

The importance of trivia

Sometimes a patient comes for counselling hoping to discover a secret formula to reconcile his and his partner's irreconcilable differences. Perhaps one partner hates that the other is untidy or can't cook or always has to be the one who is right or the first to stop an argument by slamming out of the room. The problem may have to do merely with sleeping or eating or drinking or working or religion or family relations, or something apologetically trivial but nevertheless critical. The unhappy partner wants to suppose that in therapy the relationship can be fixed by tinkering with the surface of things.

Clashes about minor differences can assume major proportions in a relationship. It is the subtle, unconscious destructive actions that two people perpetrate upon each other — a tone of voice, a turn of phrase, a contemptuous glance, a meaningful silence — that make it so difficult to calm the tumult of wills. The moment one tries to spell it out, it sounds ridiculous. The real source of the discomfort is always so much deeper, the predicament slippery, the problem elusive.

Sometimes the person engaging in the supposedly heinous conduct does not recognise his culpability when he receives the complaint, or if he does recognise it, he may be unwilling to admit to it or he may be unable to alter it. Nagging won't help if the supposed malefactor is unable to hear what is really being said or has problems elsewhere that distract his attention.

Perhaps one or both of them cannot or will not own up to their part in a miscommunication that may be difficult to describe. Going into psychotherapy, while there is no guarantee that it will magically transmute the relationship into a happy one, would be a move in a useful direction for both partners.

10

Is therapy appropriate for everyone?

Going into therapy is a strange adventure. The patient needs to be able to make a leap in the dark, to trust his therapist and surrender to the process. Psychotherapy is difficult — but possible.

Some people exclude themselves from therapy before they've tried it. It's not uncommon to hear people rejecting "Freud" without ever having read a word he wrote or without ever having sampled being in psychotherapy. They may be very distressed but will still decide on the basis of their hunch about therapy rather than knowledge about it, that it is a waste of time, or only for crazy people, or tolerable for other people but not themselves, or that the therapist is bound to be an unhelpful idiot. When they do at last go into therapy, their exploration of their reasons for their earlier delay is always interesting, as are their new ideas about it.

Psychotherapy is difficult for the patient who overvalues his level of intelligence or who isn't curious about himself. Psychotherapy is difficult for the patient who always needs to be the victim, the one who needs to blame others or a contextual circumstance or his body for his problems. Psychotherapy is difficult for the patient who absolves himself of responsibility for the course his life has taken. Psychotherapy is difficult for the patient who is too vulnerable to admit that in order for his life to be easier and happier it's not others who must change but himself. Psychotherapy is difficult for the patient who wants a quick means of undoing the unconscious learning of a lifetime, who supposes that in a handful of sessions a therapist is going to help him to seduce the new love of his life or help him to fix his marriage or help him to forego an old addiction or get rid of years of anxiety or depression.

While it is true that some people who come for just a few counselling sessions may find a quick solution to a big problem, they're often the ones who, having sampled its usefulness, return for long-term psychotherapy. They have learnt to recognise their own complexity and that their assumed problem is a symptom of something else, something subtle, deep and interesting.

Psychotherapy is useful only if the patient is able to learn to abide a state of uncertainty and can tolerate being in an imperfect relationship — with himself and with the therapist. The patient has to be able, most of the time, to trust the emotional intelligence and professionalism of the therapist; he has to be able to say if and when he doesn't and, most important, he has to want to discover why he doesn't say.

The patient who comes seeking help but who has decided in advance what form the help must take is not being contrary but, is, rather, showing his mistrust of the professional's expertise. He hardly understands what "surrendering to the process" might mean. He cannot bear to listen to his own self-critical voice chiming with the way he hears the therapist's interpretations. He cannot bear that her interpretations may chime with the feedback he gets from those who make free with proffering their opinions outside the therapy room. When at last he starts to admit to his own accountability and can perceive the therapist as working beside him and not against him, the sessions move into a different gear.

There is a contradiction here of course. We have been considering patients who make an erroneous effort to see if therapy will provide a "cure". They want their role to be as passive as it might be in the hands of a medical doctor. The same patients who at the behest of their doctor will reveal the most embarrassing bodily sites of their ailments, may baulk at revealing in words their innermost thoughts and feelings to their psychotherapist. They may also be resistant, at least for a while, to absorbing the notion that they have to face up to themselves in order to rescue themselves. The therapist is merely a quietly attentive and tentative trained facilitator, a guide towards the opportunity for the patient to think more for himself and about himself.

The blocked patient may stop looking for help altogether, or may gravitate to a workaday behavioural therapy or a quantitative cognitive therapy or an uplifting spiritual therapy or an energising physical therapy. By these means he may learn to drive underground disturbing thoughts and feelings where they don't have to be acknowledged. Such therapies are good for a temporary distraction from symptoms, for achieving the suppression of symptoms, for shifting them from a place where they show to somewhere less visible. Unfortunately, since the symptoms have not been fully excavated and confronted, they are likely to get busy elsewhere in the psyche, in a new guise.

11

Watch points for a good relationship

(a) Find out what you really want.

(b) Blame only yourself for your not getting it.

(c) Observe and manage your envy and your pride.

(d) Don't badmouth or manipulate others in order to elevate yourself.

(e) Don't try to change the other person as if you know best. Other people think they're right too.

(f) Don't stoke things up. Don't harm others or yourself. Avoid battle.

(g) Be honest, starting with yourself. Admit responsibility for your actions and take the consequences.

(h) Protect yourself. Say no or say nothing or escape an abusive situation.

(i) You may safely assume that half the time people don't have a clue who you are and the other half of the time they see right through you. It's usually a mystery which half is which.

(j) Keep things simple.

(k) Admit to yourself that good relationships require compromise exactly where you'd prefer perfection.

12

When is it love?

Trouble comes when the night he can't remember is the night she can't forget, as the inimitable Magnetic Fields sang.

Question: what are the ordinary, common signs of "being in love"?

Common answer: the fixed belief, inexplicable lust, absurd hopefulness, a starry-eyed mixture of masochism and narcissism, wishful thinking, obsessiveness indicating addiction, minute analysis of the other's communications, unreasonably high expectations of the other's positive interest, irrational and self-sacrificial decision-making for the sake of the other, alternating euphoria and despair, an assumption that the compulsion to stay connected with the other person is something called love, an expectation that the feelings are or should be reciprocated, rage or grief when they are not. In brief, a kind of madness.

Perhaps our difficulty in defining love begins with our too often leaving out the importance of love's kindness and love's reciprocity, and the importance of the difference between loving and being in love.

If someone oppresses you, frightens you, hurts you, bores you, presumes their entitlement to make demands of you on the grounds of their so-called love, then it is not love. It is need or idealisation or compulsion or exploitation. It is not love.

It is unimportant whether or not the lover says he or she loves you. It is important whether he or she has the effect of making you feel loved.

When you are not together, does the professed lover bear in mind you and your interests, your contentment and your physical well-being, you as lover and friend, perhaps parent of the children you may raise together? Is there a presumption of a long future together? Most important of all, do you reciprocate in kind?

How odd that, in contemporary society, love is expected to be a prerequisite for marriage-and-babies but it is not a prerequisite for cohabitation as husband and wife for a life-time.

13

Loneliness, mortality and the good life

We mesmerize ourselves with illusions in order to mask that not only are we here for a short span but we are here alone, grappling with our self-doubt, self-hatred, anxiety, fear, shame, guilt, despair, envy, rage, regret.

We seek to fill the solitary void in which we find ourselves. We want to be attached to something reassuring, exterior to ourselves — success or a relationship or a baby or a bigger car or a direct line to an accidental deity. We are gullible. We'll grab at anything that may seem to plug a looming gap or reverse the imminent vertigo. Some people even resort to self-destructive action, even suicide, if it seems that it will undo their panic about being insignificant in a vast universe. It is difficult to put aside one's narcissism.

The source of salvation to which we eagerly submit — whether it be the might of wealth and status, a dependable love, a protecting leader, a rewarding god — is a figment of the imagination. Our tireless search provides hallucinatory samples, fleetingly satisfying, of what we suppose will re-model our unsatisfactory reality.

Glory never comes. Rather, it comes rarely, fugaciously, mainly to deluded visionaries and psychotics. The rest of us are all ordinary mortals, mediocre, some more, some less. There is physical survival and there is virtue. The rest is vanity.

Life offers only one grand certainty and that is that not one of us escapes alive. We are born alone. We die alone. These obvious facts should be inducement enough to each of us to make the most of the time we have, not to be dragged down in disappointment because we are looking for a good life in the wrong place.

What is the secret of living a good life? Let's make the most of the ambiguity of the adjective. It's probably just as the sages have always said.

The good life is the virtuous life and the virtuous life is the fulfilled life. In other words, fulfilled life is the result of, even the reward for reducing opportunities to feel guilt, shame, panic, rage, depression, self-righteousness and narcissistic desire.

Would that we were indeed masters of ourselves. There seems once to have been a grave error of judgement: we obviously are not, after all, made in the image of God.

An imagined state of nirvana is absurdly remote. We may take comfort in that, first, we are all in this together. Second, it turns out that besides our suffering and our cruelty, far distant though we may be from nirvana, once we refrain from causing harm and hurt, a single ordinary day contains enough to marvel at for a lifetime.

14
Private distractions

We develop private and public strategies for blocking awareness of our frustration, our fear, and our acquired sense of inadequacy.

A familiar strategy for denial is to find a partner and soon have a child, a strategy which conveniently has evolved into a social norm. The relief of conforming veils the continuing unease about being aware that we are each alone.

When our strategies for induced blindness don't work, when we find that we cannot shut our eyes to our frustrating separateness from others and our dependence on others, then we feel overwhelmed and upset and may find inappropriate distractions to deny our perceptions.

Our distractions are often secret. We are self-absorbed even if not literally alone when engaged in, say, the fascination of cosmetic titillation, excesses of consumption of food, drink and drugs, or the orgasmic trance of sex. These are ordinary pleasures that remove us from the truth of our insignificant mortality. They temporarily lift the weight of our responsibility to shape our own lives and to look after others.

Ethnographic and cultural conventions may vary geographically but the psychological impact of their infraction is universal, even to the point where custom is more honoured in the breach than the observance. That is why conventions exist, to mark a tacit boundary, to create form out of formlessness.

In extreme instances there probably is trouble afoot when someone has an obsessive preoccupation with boundaries separating the private and public performance of his distracting activities or, conversely, when he shows an exaggerated disregard of those boundaries. Childish tantrums or adolescent self-regard aside, the disturbed person may not recognise a social injunction to modify his table manners in the canteen or to make less noise in a cinema or to curb his scatological speech on a bus or to refrain from bathroom grooming on the train. Every community knows when someone has breached their conventions and members of communities that live in overlapping proximities usually know how to respect and minimize their public differences. But the troubled person cannot or will not contain, for instance, the flagrant expression of his extreme emotions, cannot or will not distinguish between his local customs' private and public conduct.

These signs of despair are difficult to recognise and even when they are recognised, aren't easily addressed. For instance, men in high places who get caught in sordid ones may seem to have been self-confidently assuming their invincibility. It is more likely that they were signalling, albeit perversely, an unconscious need to put an end to their sense of isolation, to be properly seen. The subjects of these kinds of press scandals often have been suffering psychologically and emotionally and their final "self-exposure" may mean that they can accept help if it is offered in a way that doesn't make them feel worse.

15

Public distractions

Like all animals, we are social creatures. Most of us cannot bear to be alone for long. When there is another person in our vicinity, we will make small-talk to avoid being quietly with our own thoughts. We want to engage.

We are adept at imaginatively constructing substitutes to fill the lonely, empty gap. We may immerse ourselves in a passive activity with narrative content, such as a game, music, television, a movie, a book, anything to take us away from our own interior story or our suspicion that we lack one.

We develop countless means of avoiding contemplation of our own thoughts for a sustained length of time. When we cannot, we find a way to occlude the need. We invent a state of mind that simulates being with a companion or we construct surrogate company or we sedate ourselves with an opiate to empty our brains of thought - a drug or alcohol or sex or a chore or a hobby that can absorb our attention. For some, it's sleep. For the lucky ones, it's work or simply something harmless that they love to do as often as possible. Writing a book, for example.

We are easily entertained, distracted from our frustration, fear, self-doubt, self-hatred, anxiety, shame, guilt, despair, envy, rage, regret. We perk up when offered anything diverting and with no strings attached. We pay attention to anything labelled "free" ("my purse will not be violated"), "freak" ("they're weird, I'm not"), "sex" ("pleasure with minimum effort") or "drug" ("relief in lotus-land").

We happily participate by proxy as remote observers of any available spectacle, enjoying unfamiliarity, novelty, from a safe distance. When a group gives us encouragement or licence to get involved, whether it's to party or to loot or to massacre, we may throw off long-held inhibitions and join in, reserving contrition, or its denial, for later.

The presence of others in the crowd gives us the illusion of anonymity, invisibility, safety in numbers, a sense of unity with the group. We, they, become one, as collaborators, cousins, comrades. We are camouflage for each other at the party or in the skirmish. For as long as this impression lasts, this impression of merged union, of cohesion and support, we may elude our pursuing Furies, the old familiars — frustration, fear, self-doubt, self-hatred, anxiety, shame, guilt, despair, envy, rage, regret.

After the shoot-out or the act of violence, for instance, the lone perpetrator wakes up to the wretched reality of his narcissistic actions. No wonder that after his ensnared impulse to repeat his transgressions, confused and very alone, he invariably chooses to die or to hide. He prefers self-annihilation to facing the mundane truth that aside from his episodic psychosis, he is as ordinary as anyone else, including his victims.

We all like to stare at an oddity, to link the beam of our eye to an external object. We constantly search out innovation. We'll join a crowd watching a bizarre event, an extravaganza whether major or minor - people arguing in public, a traffic accident, a boring street performance, someone's outlandish get-up, an odd body. We'll gawp at anything. Adults need toy-substitutes. Those who are more needy, shop. It is all a form of play. It relieves us of our own company but unlike children at play, we do not learn much from it.

We are more likely to stop to watch a spectacle if we suppose that we are incognito, invisible, cancelled out. In certain circumstances we literally may be drawn into the spectacle itself. We may disengage from the invisible watching crowd to join the group that is watched, to become the exhibition, part of another hallucinatory experience.

Going out, we may dress up, display our attributes: we shift our source of pleasure from being the entranced to being the entrancing. We are acting out a dream, whether we are actors, terrorists, or strutters of our stuff. It is all fantastical.

Those are unusual people who as rational individuals, and not in order to become the admired exhibition, step out of the crowd in a crisis to act altruistically rather than self-indulgently. Whether or not they have institutional training in medicine or the military, especially if not, they have a rare gift that enables them spontaneously to think and act to try to save a situation from disaster or even just to stretch out a comforting hand. Witnessing their voluntary separation from the sheltering confines of the group, we regard them equally as brave and foolish. Perhaps this is what heroism is. In its simple form, it is courageous action that is focused on caring for others and minimising damage. It is the opposite of action serving as a distraction from the self.

16
Waiting, wishing and wanting

*W*aiting for someone is usually a waste of time. If you wait it probably means that you've given yourself up to someone else's schedule, or to someone else's life, or to something that doesn't even exist for you yet.

Waiting for someone is as useless as, at the opposite end of the continuum, regret about something irreparable — but at least, usually, regret implies past action and regret sometimes engages the leaven of moral conscience. Waiting is more likely to engage the two amoral poles of narcissism – unseemly self-regard and unwarranted abjection.

What are we really waiting for?

In Freud's concept of wish, an aspect of wanting, a wish is in excess of ordinary conscious yearning for something that can provide satisfaction. The individual is in a state of anticipation characterised mainly by unconscious fantasy and projection. He wants and wishes for conditions that have not and may not come to pass, except in the imagination. The granting of that wish will always be incomplete, orientating the recipient to what he or she does not have or will not get.

In a state of anticipation or regret, we are focused not on the here and now but on what we hope will come or even on what we suppose has happened in the past. At the mercy of the traces of our infantile memory, we are like babies wanting and missing the hallucination of a secure embrace at the mother's breast. We wait for something we believe we once had and long to have again: validation, security, repletion, love.

When psychoanalyst Jacques Lacan re-positioned Freud's "wish", he called it "desire". For Lacan, the subject — his version of the always complex, contradictory and incomplete person — exists in a constant state of desire. That's how we all are, what we all do. In one way or another the subject is always desiring an object, desiring a would-be construction that corresponds to a notion of something or someone other, something or someone supposedly other than itself. By definition, the object of desire is always out of reach because once it is attained it ceases to be out of reach: the subject is driven to focus on another object of desire. Desire precedes its object.

One can wait, wish, regret, for as long as one likes but desire will never be satisfied permanently, whether it's the desire of the toddler demanding ice-cream or the desire of a decrepit president who refuses to resign or the desire of the newlywed haunted by inexpressible unease. We've all heard a parent in a toy shop or at the sweet-counter shouting, unbearably, at a child, "Stop nagging! Stop saying 'I want this, I want that'!" The tone of the interdiction is horribly familiar to us. We empathise with the irate parent and we also identify with the controlled, frustrated, desiring child.

The object of desire is myriad. The child doesn't stop whinging vocally until he is old enough to internalise his speech, old enough to transmute his demands into the tempting or admonishing inner dialogue of what Freud's translator termed the "id" and the "superego". These are conflicting parts of our unconscious that impel our conduct and then pass sentence upon it from a position of power.

In the drive towards a satisfaction of desire, the end point never arrives, satisfaction can never be fully arrived at. The desirous creature can never stop at last and say, "Now I have it." Only the goalposts may be moved.

*

Desire persists, attaching itself to new objects. The nescient gunman who finds that he must murder all who supposedly obstruct his unreachable goal is akin to a boy-soldier in a region of military conflict groomed from youth to know only the meanest slither of the world. He serves as cannon fodder in the war-games, the half-realised, desiring, distant fantasies of phallic domination, the fantasies of older men who authorise military deployment from a safe distance, outsource the danger to themselves, ruling over those who risk death for them. Those who risk death for their elders are feeding their own fantastical desire to be a band of brothers, each at last a beloved of the unreachable parent.

The fiends that terrorise the terrorist's own thoughts are his anxiety about his helplessness, a childlike fear of annihilation for wrong-doing, of punishment, even annihilation, for indulging his desire. Inscribed within his murderous actions are his feelings of inadequacy, guilt, shame, fear of being humiliated, the threat of being un-manned by symbolic or actual castration.

Needing to mark out the boundaries of his psychological safety, this young person the more easily learns to channel the body's desires, his own or another's. He projects on to others, accuses and punishes others for having his own disturbing, disowned feelings of lawless, erotically-charged disarray. He is threatened with his own annihilation by the very figure of authority who offers a means to transmute his desires from private self-persecution to public reward – some time in the future.

The dénouement for the young aggressor trapped on this treadmill must perforce be his own violent death, its inevitable horror denied or assuaged by promises that he can't test because their fulfilment is in an imagined afterlife.

*

Living a full, free life attempting not to hurt anyone, including oneself, entails the management of desire and the direction of its energy away from destructiveness. One needs to find a way to live fairly with difference. Unfortunately, whether in the conflict of a war zone or the conflict of a relationship, the process cannot be unilaterally controlled because it must be reciprocal.

Reluctantly, we have to grow up and find ways to survive the reality of rarely getting our own way.

Maturity means being able to distinguish between one's inner wishes and one's impulse to force others to fulfil them. Maturity means coming to terms with the fact that one cannot control the thoughts or desires of other people. Maturity means discovering what one wants, which is hard enough, and then, the catch, learning to acknowledge that in a healthy society one cannot have everything one wants.

17
Women's liberation

The women's movement has done wonders but, sadly, most women's intellectual liberation is ahead of their emotional liberation.

It's not unusual for a single woman who says she is appalled by sexism to baulk at asking a man she fancies to go on a date. Indeed, lest he think she is too eager, she will even hide her interest in him, sometimes so well that he gets the impression that she is avoiding him. Meanwhile, if he doesn't reply to her last email, she will search for the meaning of his silence, scour the social media for signs of his interests elsewhere and wait in agonies for his phone-call. After they've spoken she will analyse the significance of his every phrase. She will be hurt if he shows insufficient interest in her, as if her preoccupation with him legitimises her expectation that he respond in kind.

She would do well to explore the disjunction between the sexist values she abhors and her emotional responses to the man she desires or to the man who does not reciprocate with his desire of her. There is a fault-line at the junction of her lust, her would-be socialised self, her evolutionary hard-wiring, and her low self-esteem.

Paradoxically, despite describing herself as the equal of men, she will be offended or even feel threatened if a man leers at her. She will be outraged, even hurt, if he directs at her his antediluvian sexism. Her outrage, fear, offence or hurt are responses incompatible with self-assured equality with men.

If a man man-handles a woman in a social setting, lays hands upon her inappropriately, literally or figuratively in speech, it is only her sexist conditioning that prevents her from naming and shaming him in the moment, out loud, and in public. Yes, there is the initial shock that renders one silent but girls and women had best encourage each other to learn the difficult lesson of standing up for oneself in the moment.

Since everything in our societies across the globe conspires to silence women, this is of course a big ask. Fortunately in the West, unfortunately not entirely, the law entitles women to assert their equality.

*

We have not been referring to physical assault or rape. These belong to a different category of violation. It seems reasonable to distinguish here between the ubiquity of the ordinary, stupid sexism and exceptional personal circumstances where a woman finds herself trapped in the horror of physical threats or actual abuse by someone bigger and stronger than her, a man.

While these scenarios are born of the same sexism, the means by which a woman may learn to deal with them are qualitatively different. There is the category that includes a girl or woman's reasonable psychological self-assertion in the family, the home and the work-place, and then there is the category that includes physical and emotional maltreatment at the hands of would-be masculine thugs. It would be useful if feelings of being offended could be put aside in favour of some clarity about whether the man's sexist conduct is risible or criminal, whether he should be made the butt of a joke or the recipient of a prison sentence.

Unfortunately, our so-called liberated, egalitarian, democratic society does absolutely nothing to train girls to deal with either of these linked categories. Nor does it train men to eschew their perpetuation.

Every day every woman is on the receiving end of ordinary sexism. These instances, large and small, are merely evidence of men's destructive attempts to mask their simultaneous fear and need of women. Until women can respond with asperity, humour or indifference, it will remain a man's world.

Women ultimately will only be free of the yoke of all manifestations of sexism when we find the emotional, social and psychological means to make ourselves economically independent of men. This will require a cooperative way of managing the consequences of being the child-bearers and the primary care-givers. It will require a new way of managing love and sex in our lives.

18
Obsessive love

Obsessive feelings for a person are driven by forms of love and hate. They express an addiction to another person, or, more accurately, an addiction to a fanciful idea of that person. The addict occupies a place on the narcissistic continuum where he (or she) either over-values or under-values himself particularly in relation to the focus of his obsession.

Obviously not all secret stalkers are the mentally ill dangerous criminals we hear of in the news. It is not unusual to learn that someone has found himself or herself temporarily driven to trace the uninterested or unsuspecting object of his desire. The common practice of tracking someone's activities via social media is an example of the current normalising of intrusiveness. People talk unashamedly about investigating someone on social media and of course the primary if not obligatory aim of those media is to facilitate their participants' social exposure. Nevertheless, the tracked-down person is often unaware of the identity or motive of those to whom they are revealed, albeit usually with a neutral or benign outcome.

Snout

Let's take the example of someone we'll call Snout. He (but it could as well be a she) finds it impossible to face the likelihood of his love object's probable disinterest and hopes that eventually his feelings will be reciprocated. He is swept away by his flight of fancy, a mini-mania resembling the opposite of paranoia. He supposes that all he needs is the air-time to enlighten his quarry of what is on offer and what she will miss if she refuses him.

Snout believes that he will win over the object of his desire if he can just discover — better still, if she will just tell him — what will please her, what she wants. He just needs the magic words from her, the golden key, the secret signal that will effect the transformation of his status from locked out to let in. He torments himself trying to discover just the right formulation of words, the right nuance of gesture, the right side to part his hair, the right time to say the right thing. The moment is always just out of reach, ahead of him, like Gatsby's green light across the water. His delusory, wishful state just about succeeds in fending off despair. Soon all will be his.

Snout keeps trying, keeps tracking, keeps longing. Because of the supposed imminence of the love object's expected metamorphosis, or annunciation, or revelation, and provided he has been lucky enough already to have homed in on his target, Snout is compelled to analyse every phone-call, text or email from his beloved for its hidden meaning, for its certain promise of her transfiguration from beloved to lover. His unwarranted, hyper-alert optimism, exhausts him, "drives him crazy". Meanwhile, he probably can't bring himself to ask her a straight question because he is afraid of getting a straight answer — in the negative. His show must go on.

Snout eventually starts seeing a therapist. He comes not for help in examining whether or not his obsessive pursuit of this love object is fanatical or fantastical. He comes because he wants expert advice about why his success is so slow in coming and what he should do in order to make the other person want him, to see things his own way. He wants to find out how to manipulate his object of desire in order to satisfy his desire. He wants to use the therapy to further his obsessive aim. He can't accept that the object of his affection shows no sign of reciprocating his feelings and his problem is not failure but self-delusion.

Snout doesn't regard his conduct as manipulative. Manipulation suggests malign intent and he is in love and wishes only the best for his beloved: he wishes her possession of himself. He doesn't doubt that he knows better than she what is good for her. His difficulty, he believes, is in persuading her of his superior wisdom.

He is unable to see her as a separate person with a mind of her own, a person who will do her own choosing. The reason that he can't see her separateness is precisely because of it. The evidence of her separateness he interprets as the evidence of her ignorance, from his point of view: she doesn't see that he is the man for her. Meanwhile, he, of course, knows what is good for her, he believes. He is unable to grasp that she is as complex as himself, far too complex to be changed in a long-lasting way just because someone about whom she doesn't care wants her to change, wants her to care about him.

One can imagine scenarios where a person who is an obsessed person's object of desire is compelled to submit by the use of physical threats, or is bought in some way, with money or by means of a cultural exchange of some kind, as in a forced marriage. The resulting conjunction won't be an unencumbered pleasure because it is not driven by reciprocated desire. It won't have the characteristics that the stalker first adored in his fantasy. For the person who is his object of desire, there is no pleasure in having been dragooned into being an object, a thing.

19
The absent partner

Hermia and Hermes

A young woman, whom we shall call Hermia, was a train-driver, active in her union, successful in a domain with few women at her level. She was confident, attractive, energetic, single. She described herself as self-sufficient in every respect. She was pleased that any man whom she had ever dated had never had to suspect her of wanting to exploit him for his money or his eligibility or his sperm count. He could be sure that she was with him because she wanted to be with him for himself.

About six months into her new relationship with, let's call him Hermes, for several reasons she decided to see a counsellor. She was keen to spell out her new boyfriend's positive attributes.

She said that one of the reasons she got on well with Hermes was that, unusually, while he disliked his work as a shop assistant, he did not turn that into energy to undermine her own success at work. He was not competitive with her. He accepted that her job preoccupied her and took up a lot of her time. He wasn't threatened by the pleasure she took in her work or her status in the profession. Indeed, he respected her for it. She said that in her experience this was unusual in the men whom she had dated in the past.

Despite the many positives in their relationship, there was a problem. She felt that when they were together, he wasn't quite "with" her. What did she mean? She said he wasn't intimate with her. She was not referring to their sexual relationship, which she said was good, but to the way he spoke to her about himself. He didn't talk about troubles at work, he didn't discuss his parents or siblings, he didn't meander into disclosure about his past or share with her his future hopes. He didn't talk about his emotions or comment on ordinary incidents in his life or gossip with her about people they knew. He didn't "let her in", was how she put it. She couldn't get close.

Was Hermia revealing obliquely that she suspected that Hermes didn't really want a permanent relationship with her? No, it wasn't that: she said that more than once he had talked about the children they would have one day and he always assumed that their relationship would continue.

She said in her therapy sessions that he may have wanted to live with her for the rest of their lives but she felt that she didn't know who he was. She decided to tell him.

Hermes immediately tried to correct his apparent failing. He revealed a secret about his parents that he had never told anybody. While she understood his intention, his confiding a family secret didn't address the problem she had with him which was that in their own interactions she felt that he withheld himself from her.

She was stymied. What should she do in order to get him to relax with her, to open up, to trust her, to be himself with her?

But what if his manner with her was not to be taken personally, was not a clue to his level of commitment to the relationship? It was possible that the guarded, inexpressive man whom she described as her partner simply was what Hermes was like. She couldn't accept that possibility.

She said that she could feel him withholding a part of his personality from her, her in particular. She noticed how different he was when she was not present, when he was just with his men friends. With them he was lively, vocal, spontaneous.

At this juncture we cannot but note that her observation had a hole in it. How did she know what he was like when she was absent? Her description of her accessing the information was so vague that it seemed possible that she secretly recorded his conversations with his men friends or somehow accessed his communications without his knowing. Perhaps she felt too guilty to admit to her therapist how she had arrived at her insight into what he was like when she wasn't present.

Our sessions continued, covering material from several areas of her life including the ever-present but somehow ever-absent Hermes.

As the weeks went by, I noticed three or four minor occasions on which Hermia lied to me.

They were incidental mendacities, ostensibly external to our therapy work and spectacularly banal. She tied herself up in opaque elucidation about, say, explanations for missed payments or unreasonable reasons for having to re-schedule an appointment. As far as I could make out, she gained nothing by being dishonest with me.

Between the therapist and the patient, questions of honesty are fundamental. Because so much of psychotherapy and counselling involves working with defence mechanisms entailing forms of denial, therapists can develop good radar for detecting untruths while, of course, it's not always relevant to point out every instance that is detected.

What information was embedded in Hermia's trivial infractions?

On the one hand, she presented herself to the world as a capable, independent woman who could hold her own socially and professionally in what is called a man's world. On the other, her lies seemed to be meant to serve as a cover for small mistakes, as if she was anticipating a verdict and a sentence for a wrongful act even though the wrongful act was, by anyone standards, paltry.

Perhaps her lies were a variety of hiding. They inadvertently disclosed a version of her as a little girl afraid of being seen and judged, a child who supposes that if she hides her head under a pillow of obfuscations, she can't be seen and so won't be judged. Paradoxically, she had trapped herself in a self-reflexive Möbius strip. The wrongful act was the very lie Hermia had to tell in order to escape the imagined punishment that supposedly would follow her having told the lie in the first place.

If in her secret inner world Hermia felt hemmed in by looming danger, it was no surprise that her highly-strung, super-woman demeanour masked, not very well, childlike panic. Her working life, what we may summarise as the masculine part of her, was crammed with exhausting hours of employment, with adroit, stressful negotiations and knife-edge decisions.

All that was as nothing compared to the exposed, hazardous plains of the precarious, Escher-esque world that Hermia's unconscious required she inhabit. She was driven to protect her own vulnerability and to hide from what she imagined was looming judgement and punishment at the hands of a greater power. Inwardly feeling like a child, she needed to remain distant from the threatening gaze of any adult. No surprise, she had selected a boyfriend whose default position was to remain as distant as possible from his sexual partner, or perhaps women in general.

Presumably Hermia fibbed to Hermes too and presumably her fibs were nothing to him. She had chosen someone sufficiently disengaged from intimate emotion with his girlfriend that she was always safely remote from the verdict and sentence he might otherwise pronounce upon her.

It seemed likely that as long as she avoided examining the secrets that she tried to keep from herself, and as long as she had to lie about inconsequentialities, she would always feel and actually be ostracised. She was not merely imagining that she was excluded from the emotional life of the man with whom she – ostensibly – wanted to spend the rest of her days. She really was shut out.

20
On being besotted

Constance and Curtis

Let's consider a situation in which a woman, we'll call her Constance, is enamoured of a man, let's call him Curtis. (Obviously we can reverse the genders or keep them the same but for simplicity's sake we'll do it this way.) So — a certain woman is crazy about a certain man.

Perhaps Constance thinks that Curtis is the most attractive man in her circle of friends or work-place or college. Curtis may not even know of Constance's existence. She may not even be a flicker of interest in his mind's eye but in her own mind's eye she is designing her wedding dress and he's wheeling their baby's carriage across their lawn. Her infatuation inscribes an arc of events starting with a wish that she stands a chance with him. Her wish becomes a belief that she does.

Let us suppose that Constance does indeed enter his field of vision. By this stage, even if she is the most self-possessed, intelligent, independent of people, the chances are that if Curtis gives her the opportunity, she will surrender to him and will want to believe that they are therefore connected to each other, a couple in formation. He may demonstrate clearly that her feelings are not reciprocated but this will not repel her. Curtis may ignore her phone-calls, he may forget their dinner-dates, he may flirt with someone else in front of her, he may perform any number of deeds that demonstrate that he isn't worried about souring her feelings for him but it won't put her off him. She will find excuses for what would be inconsiderate conduct if they were a couple in love, which they are not. Continuing the flimsy connection with him is more important to her than listening to her rational self, more important to her than letting him know that he has hurt her, more important to her than risking the consequences of attending to what stares her in the face.

He betrays no impulse to make an effort to

give her pleasure. He doesn't notice or doesn't care when she feels rejected, ignored, even abused. He shows no interest in nurturing their bond presumably because from his point of view there is none. In parallel, she hides that she's hurt, hides it especially from herself.

A person who is besotted with someone is often unable to protect her self-respect. Our love-sick Constance, far from discarding the inconsiderate Curtis - disturbingly near but so elusive - may subject herself to even more pain in her determination to win him over or, in some sense, to keep him. He may not be aware of how hard she tries to please him not least because she hides her heartache. He may believe that she isn't especially perturbed when, say, he doesn't turn up for an arrangement they've made. Constance probably invents a story to tell him that masks her upset, a story such as that she didn't turn up herself, or that she and her friends didn't wait around long for him and went on to a party without him. Curtis may well be taken in and suppose that he, in return, wasn't much considered and wasn't missed.

Constance doesn't want him to know the

emotion that his indifference arouses in her. She doesn't want him to know that she waited for him to arrive and worried for a long time, imagining him either in a car crash or, worse, with another woman. Curtis won't know that she spent the night weeping, that her fabrications are her attempts not to alienate him from her, that she is in love with him,

He likes her but is not in love with her. Aside from two or three drunken nights when his intoxication, "obviously" not himself, may have whispered sweet nothings, he has never pretended that he wants a long-term association with her. This is not because he's a callous cad exploiting her but rather because she just isn't much on his mind. Her image doesn't slip of its own accord into his reveries. He certainly never ruminates upon what he'll wear on their wedding day or how soon they can have a baby, lax though he may be about ensuring that he doesn't impregnate her.

21
When good sex is bad news

If one partner's battered self-esteem directs proceedings, he or she may try harder to please, as if the other partner's disregard is justified. Trying harder to please may entail becoming the domestic skivvy or pretending there isn't infidelity or fetishising their sex life or a lot else.

The abject partner often suffers from the delusive supposition that good sex means that deep down his or her love is reciprocated. In reality, it may be or it may not be. Meanwhile, she (if it is a woman, though it could equally be a man) sees great promise in their erotic symbiosis and supposes that it signals a long-term happy outcome.

She supposes that, given that the sex is good, he will treat her more lovingly if she can just correct her failings that must be the cause, outside the bedroom, of his frequent disappointing disregard of her. His apparent failings do not deflect her from her optimism. She assumes that later on, once he has chosen her and thus, she supposes, he is in her possession, she will have a chance to correct what she doesn't like about him.

There is no end to the temporary blindness that love-and-sex can induce. Any number of people go even as far as marrying each other while assuming or at least hoping that in the future their mismatched values and interests will alchemise into marital harmony as honey-sweet as their present sex life. Unfortunately, while the passing of time makes changes, wishing doesn't make magic.

An enamoured person cannot understand that the quality of the sex and the endearments that he whispers to her while the sex is happening are independent of his opinion about spending the rest of his life with her. The possibility of cohabitation or marriage, uppermost in her mind, may or may not cross his. That it never crosses his mind is inconceivable to her, swept away as she is by their exceptionally satisfying physical fit.

If he never mentions marriage, it is surely up to her, she supposes, to interpret the clues that he drops in order for her to find out what he thinks about it.

While marriage may never cross his mind at all, he may still want to continue the relationship for as long as possible — on his own terms.

22
The anxiety of possession

While there is always something ridiculous about making rigid generalisations about gender, we may as well concede that anecdotally evident truisms in our culture often turn out to be statistically accurate. So often one can scratch the surface to find the notion corroborated that while biological gender is not necessarily identical with social or psychological gender, there are nevertheless consistent patterns in the different aims in the relationships of men and women.

Even a staunch feminist may spend far more time than a man would spend in imagining her future with a man whom she has met only recently. Men's fantasies of the future are often fairly well grounded in a version of reality, first structured around work, money and enhancing their self-image and status, and second, around the next pleasure point, be it the next promotion or the next pint or the next carnal encounter.

The masculine fantasy (and obviously biological genders are interchangeable) tends towards securing symbolic indicators of power and status. In contrast, the feminine fantasy focuses on acquiring a haven in which to be, literally or figuratively, a wife and a mother, whether this is achieved symbolically as the CEO of a corporation or by reigning over the dishwashing rota in the house-share or by finding a house-mate who plays masculine protector by, say, standing surety for the lease.

In the commitment stakes, a young man in the early stages of an encounter with a woman tends not to think as far ahead as his female counterpart. He is inclined to focus on his sexual desirability in the woman's eyes and her satisfaction of his urge to feel better about himself as a sexual creature— right now.

Once they have declared a commitment to each other, as long as she is sexually available to him, the man will relax and feel better about himself: he has accomplished his mission.

Although it may be disputed by some women

who have been victims of domestic violence, it seems that generally as long as the partner in the masculine position perceives his partner as belonging to him, he is *not* particularly sexually suspicious or jealous. He may have uncomfortable moments but he is not easily roused to distrust her if she treats him unkindly or is admired by other men. As long as he knows that she is his, which usually means that as long as she voluntarily has sex with him, he can contain his reactions to salvos upon his completeness as a man in possession of a woman.

A man overwhelmed with sexual jealousy seems to occupy something of the feminine position. His jealous rage against her barely conceals what is really his rage against himself for his need of her to complete him. He rages against himself for feeling castrated, rendered powerless by her separateness from him.

A woman who suspects that her hold on her partner is tenuous may be overwhelmed with uncertainty about his faithfulness, sexual jealousy. For this reason, she needs the reassurance provided by his displays of affection outside as well as inside the bedroom.

23
Love as addiction

Gertrude and Grumio

Traditional literature is full of epic tales of spurned, ardent lovers who at last win over their beloved by virtue of their persistence, a persistence which literature doesn't call addiction. Today we might.

Consider the example of a woman (or man) who continues to love a man (or woman) when he has already decisively turned away from her.

A young teacher, let's call her Gertrude, had been emotionally wounded several times by different men whom she had loved and cared for. They were of a familiar type, she said, the type of men who take and take while she, as she saw it, would be giving and giving. Eventually it would all end in tears and recrimination. This pattern seemed to be repeating itself again in her latest relationship so she decided to try something different and sought out therapy.

She had been involved with a young man, let's call him Grumio, an actor whom she had loved for several months and who at first appeared to reciprocate her feelings. Then he accepted a small part in a musical. It came with a reliable contract to tour the country with the show for nearly a year. Not only did he end his relationship with Gertrude but he refused to have further contact with her.

She could see no reason for his coming to this drastic decision. She persisted in believing, and informed him repeatedly, that he had made a terrible mistake. If he would just give her the chance, she could persuade him to see that they were soul-mates and that they should spend the rest of their lives together.

Although Grumio was explicit about not wanting to stay in touch with her and, conveniently, was constantly moving digs, lodging in different towns far afield, Gertrude continued by various ingenious strategies to maintain intermittent contact with him. Some of her sequences of communication appeared to be justified. How could she get back the sun-hat she'd left in his car? Didn't she still owe him money for the festival tickets he'd paid for? Someone they'd once met at a party had asked her to ask him something, and so on. In addition, there were her countless texts, emails, quaint postcards and little postal gifts expressing her undying adoration of him, to none of which he responded.

A turning point came when she found out the town where the musical was next showing and she took a train there. She was waiting for him near the theatre's stage door when he was due to arrive for that evening's performance. Grumio spotted her in good time and set off smartly in the opposite direction. The clutch of fans waiting to glimpse the arrival of the stars of the musical were entertained by the unexpected side-show of Gertrude's vocal barrage and her sprint in pursuit of the fleeing swain.

She was gym fit and kept up with him, lugging her overnight bag, shouting at him to stop being ridiculous and to notice her. Still refusing to acknowledge her, at last he changed course and loped back to the theatre, miserably pretending to ignore her diatribe about his cold-bloodedness, her love of him and their being made for each other. At the stage door, two crew members came to Grumio's rescue, prised her off him, hauled him inside and shut the door on her.

Seeing the shell-shocked stares of the fans gathered there, as Gertrude reported it, had the effect of a slap in the face. She was suddenly aware of the noise she had been making and the silence when she recovered her senses. A taxi drew up just then to drop off someone. She cried all the way back to the station where she took the next train home.

Later, in a therapy session, she recounted the scene with some humour but she admitted that at the time she was frighteningly out of control, could not stop herself. After all the love she had given Grumio, his aggressive and cruel conduct was incomprehensible to her. It was true that she had been over-emotional, persistent, even embarrassing, but his heartlessness was shocking. He had treated her as if she were a stranger, not someone with whom he had shared tender, loving days and nights. Her outrage and anguish in the face of his steely silence, the way he had batted away her hand each time she reached out to him, had wrested from her all inhibition, had made her mad, she said.

Many months later, well into the therapy and long after she had last seen him, when her outward relations with men had become more grounded and when she was now in a stable relationship with another man, she confided that she still thought lovingly of Grumio. If only he had given her a chance to explain to him the rare quality of their connection, if only he had listened to her, then it would be he who was her fiancé, not the man she was with.

There was still psychotherapeutic work to be done but, fortunately for all of them, she had found the wherewithal to refrain from acting out her fantasies about Grumio. She could contain them, however sadly, where they belonged: in her imagination.

24
Hope v. expectation

Thaisa and Trinculo

Here's a variation on the example of someone muddling up what she hopes for with the likelihood of it actually happening.

A woman, let's call her Thaisa, is very keen on a man she's recently started dating, let's call him Trinculo. She is astonished and delighted when very soon after they've met, he suggests that they take off a fortnight from work and go on a famously extravagant cruise. Despite the newness of their liaison and her own substantial reservations about him, she presumes this means, as she puts it, that "he is serious about the relationship". A week later they have a raging argument and she realises that he's not for her.

She decides not only to refuse his holiday invitation but to bring their association to an immediate end.

On reflection, she decides to give it another chance. Perhaps the relationship has too much going for it to give up on it so quickly. Perhaps once they are relaxing in the lap of luxury, they'll be able to focus just on each other. Also, this kind of treat may never be offered to her again and it would be silly to forego the opportunity just because they had an argument. At no point does it occur to Thaisa that a man who pays for an expensive holiday so soon after meeting a woman might be sexually desperate or exploiting her greed or buying her, or all three.

Soon they embark on their voyage. Her unhappiness with him persists, exacerbated by the contrast with the pleasure-fest available to them. To add to her woes, while she had supposed that the holiday was to be paid for by Trinculo, after a few days on the boat it becomes evident to her that not merely must she contribute her share of expenses during the trip but that he assumes she's going to reimburse him for what he has already paid out for her ticket.

She is forced to admit to herself that he never said in so many words that he would pay for her holiday, that it was his treat. Worse, recalling conversations they had had, she suspects that as their date of departure approached he must have become aware of her misunderstanding but he just let her suppose what she wanted to suppose until well after they had embarked.

She is only too aware that later she will feel the financial pinch very badly. Not only is she shocked and disappointed but she is humiliated: it seems to her that he had the last laugh. He had enticed her to join him by allowing her to presume that he was paying for her but then he got her for free.

Curiously, the effect of the shock is to make her more determined than ever that the relationship work, as if she will get something back from him in the future if it does.

Initially Thaisa's vanity had been flattered by what she supposed would be a luxurious gift from Trinculo. She had liked the sound of her own voice recounting her triumph to her friends and colleagues. When she had supposed that he would pay for everything, she had felt guiltless about exploiting his high income. She said in her therapy sessions that she knew of women who remained with husbands whom they despised for the single reason that divorce would mean lowering the standard of living to which they had become accustomed. Since that motivation to stay in a relationship was regarded as socially acceptable, indeed, "normal", what was wrong with her having accepted, as she'd thought, the gift of an expensive holiday from a new boyfriend? While Thaisa said that she felt no shame about having made an unethical choice, secretly she was furious with Trinculo for his mean trickery.

She did not divulge any of these views to her friends or even to Trinculo. The relationship staggered along with six months of ups and downs. Thaisa became used to having a partner. They had a history of shared experiences, had met and liked each other's friends and family. The only problem for her was that she just didn't like him. We can only guess at what he thought of her.

Things finally came to an end for the same reasons she had given before the cruise. She recognised that she could have saved herself a great deal of unhappiness, not to mention time and money, had she followed her gut instinct right at the start and had kept an eye on the morality of her actions.

While it is easy to point a finger at Thaisa's vanity and greed, there was a much more powerful inducement for her to ignore her reason telling her to end the relationship soon after it began. This was her optimistic vulnerability, a part of her that harboured the fantastical wish that an unhappy relationship can turn into a good one. Her expedient thoughts aside, she had genuinely hoped that on the cruise, in a new context and without the familiar stresses of home and work, the two of them could start the relationship afresh. A part of her had innocently expected to find, after all her initial uncertainty about Trinculo, that he would reveal himself as not just rich but also kind and generous, someone whom she could love. The child in her supposed that she could kiss the frog and it would turn into a prince.

We all know that we take ourselves with us wherever we go and also that a new context produces its own tribulations. Even had there been an enchanting transformation while Thaisa and Trinculo were on holiday, as couples often report happens, on their return home, as couples also report, the enchantment usually disappears along with the romantic setting. As it turned out, for these two there was little enchantment before, during or after.

In matters of love and sex it is difficult to find it in ourselves to listen to reason, not least our own reason. Why is it so difficult? There are powerful evolutionary, biological, physical and sexual forces at play, all of them unconscious.

To resist self-destructive attraction one needs to be able to look after one's own moral and physical welfare just as a good adult carer looks after a child. One needs to learn not to *be* the child.

25
The accused

Many people persuade themselves that they are in the right and that if there is a problem in their relationship it is the fault of the other person. Given half a chance they will describe to anyone who cares to listen the several ways in which their partner warrants accusation.

This does not preclude these same critical individuals from feeling constantly guilty and inadequate in the relationship. At the same time as they complain about their partner, they themselves feel in some profound sense "in the wrong".

Are they right or are they wrong?

26
The unhappy child within

Guilt, blame and low self-esteem all issue from the same place in the psyche, a place located on the continuum of narcissism.

If you feel that too often someone offends you or that you don't get the respect due to you or too often you feel useless and stupid or too often you blame others or too often you exonerate yourself from blame, then you are addressing matters to do with your low self-esteem.

Low self-esteem is an unfounded, uncalled-for notion of, paradoxically, your self-importance. It is a notion self-constructed on the basis of ideas that seem to be imposed on you, that you adopt as if they were your own ideas and as if they were true. You are policing yourself and passing judgment upon yourself according to the values of others, mainly remembered versions of individuals you have known, who once seemed to or actually did disparage you.

The people offending you in the present may or may not intend to. Your projection on to them presumes their intention. If they indeed deliberately offend you or cause you discomfort, reflect upon the reason that you do not remove yourself from their company. If a person makes you feel unhappy, whether or not that person is conscious of their effect, consider why you continue to present yourself to that person as a voluntarily and constantly replenished receptacle of unhappy feelings – probably theirs to begin with.

What is the reason that you do not discover your own best emotional interests and then seek to gain it?

An essential and very difficult exercise is to explore what you gain by inflicting punishment on yourself, though the other may wield the whip, by remaining in the orbit of those who distress you.

Is it possible that you lodge yourself in Punishment Place in order to avoid a worse punishment elsewhere? If so, this habit could be prompted by a threat that no longer exists, say, the childhood recollection of being trapped in a vicious circle, of being regularly persecuted for trying to ward off persecution. Or perhaps the recollection is of arousing the envy of someone whom you think wants or once wanted you to fail, someone who can't now or once couldn't bear that others think well of you? Or was there once someone to whom it simply did not occur to bother about you or to notice you, so you stayed in place, even where you were abused, trying harder to win their fond regard? Because a version of the child we each once were is alive within us, early habituation, accidental childhood training, is difficult to undo. (Undoing it is the stuff of psychotherapy.)

There is no safe place to which a child can escape. An abused or unhappy child, perforce trapped in the family circumstance, often does his best to please or placate the punitive adult in the vain hope of diminishing the magnitude of the attacks upon him. The pattern is the same as that of an adult trapped in an abusive relationship.

Your low self-regard may be your way of

making yourself small, of even playing dead, in order not to rouse the envy or revenge or maltreatment of an imagined version of a person who used to look after their own interests at your expense.

The only way out of the trap is to find it in yourself to test whether the punishment you work so hard to avoid is inevitable and would be as intolerable as you suppose it would be.

If you have done the tests and have found that the punishment is utterly intolerable to you, it may be worth questioning the reasonableness of your finding it so: after all, you are no longer quite that same child.

27

Pressure points

Many people suppose that members of a family, those around them who share a genetic or emotional or sexual relationship, are automatically subject to rules of obligation to each other. For example, they suppose that your family or partner should love and protect you. In return you offer faithful allegiance to your family or partner. For this reason, they assume, in the case of a transgression or wayward behaviour, your family or partner would support you, grant you leeway, understanding, concessions, indulgence, forgiveness, help.

On the contrary, unless your partner or family group is threatened from the outside, it seems that the rule tends the other way. Group members have strict expectations of each other and may be ruthlessly unforgiving when their expectations are not met. Consider in your own recent past an occasion when you were in a big disagreement with a partner or a member of your family. Were you given leeway, understanding, concessions, indulgence, forgiveness and help?

A partner or each family member presumes they are owed a debt or are in debt to another, morally or emotionally or financially. There is hurt or outrage when someone professes ignorance of or resistance to paying what is owed. The debt and payment can be trivial or profound, can range from mopping the floor to putting up with physical abuse to being forbidden intimacy with someone of your own choosing. There seems to be no limit to what one person may feel entitled to ask of another within the family. In some cultures it may go as far as physical abuse or mutilation, forced marriage, murder, or a lifetime of emotional abuse.

Problems arise when there is a disjunction between one person's expectation and another's satisfaction. Perhaps someone subject to certain expectations about his conduct is, or pretends to be, ignorant of those expectations. Perhaps he acknowledges them but opposes them. Perhaps he assumes that the other's expectations are justified and he suffers, guiltily, for being unable to meet them.

There's the man who believes he doesn't earn enough money to buy everything his children deserve. There's the woman who fears she isn't attractive to her husband. There's the son who keeps failing his exams and disappointing his parents. There's the girl who believes she has disgraced herself and her family by losing her virginity before marriage.

Coping mechanisms may hide psychological pain but then they can spawn compensatory actions. Using our last example, we see that the man who believes he doesn't earn enough money to buy everything his children deserve is the man who gambles away the little he has. The woman who fears that she isn't attractive to her husband is the woman who can't control her weight. The son who keeps failing his exams and disappointing his parents is the son whose devotion to sport or to playing truant is his excuse for not doing schoolwork. The girl who believes she has disgraced herself and her family by losing her virginity before marriage is the girl who becomes depressed or anorexic or sexually promiscuous. These are examples of attempts to cope with guilt, to deny it, assuage it, project it on to another person. The effect is to spread a plague of new complexities through existing relationships.

The difficult question presented to people who are suffering within their familiar orbit is whether the protection given by the family, or the collective's cultural arbiters, outweighs the hardship of being cast out of the demanding, familial, or familiar, sanctum.

28
Not knowing

*D*espite what romantic convention has to say about pining suitors and hard-hearted women, it seems that it is more often women (or partners in the female position) than men (or partners in the male position) who consciously submit to unrequited love.

Of course one may cite plenty of exceptions: men may also surrender to a relationship where they are loved less than they love or where they are not loved at all. Generally, to continue generalizing, men don't repeatedly, as women may, articulate it thus. Men don't usually express the pain of not having their love requited, or less often see it as quite the impediment to an adequate relationship that women see it as. Men often seem to be able to submit to unrequited love without fully owning that that is what they are doing.

A person who occupies the masculine position in a relationship seems to be less susceptible to the annihilating anguish that a woman will feel upon, say, discovering that she's been used as a one-night-stand by someone she trusted, or, in another case, when after many years of marriage she discovers how little respect her partner has for her. Women, or rather those in the feminine position, seem more susceptible than men to the unhappiness caused by discovering that they aren't loved or aren't respected in the way they imagine they should be.

Perhaps men's resilience has to do with their access to compensatory activities, for instance, society being lenient with men taking sexual liberties outside the partnership. Women are not as readily indulged. And perhaps there is an explanation to be found in a girl's early childhood experience of girlishness. Girls receive a long pre-feminist training in abjection and submission each time that they observe grown women accepting scraps of regard, each time that they observe that the patronising treatment of females is the norm.

We have to bear in mind that boys are brought up mainly by women. Something in these gender relations later has its effect in the love stakes, often making grown men more resilient, less jealous, less paranoid, less suspicious than grown women. This is not to say that men don't have these feelings but the feelings don't seem to hover near the surface as they do with women. Men perhaps find ways outside the relationship to compensate for their feelings of abandonment, isolation and vulnerability.

Many love relationships begin with this same pattern, if a slightly less melodramatic version of it: the partner in the female position is constantly anxious about the level of "commitment" felt by the partner in the male position. The anxiety is fueled by a compulsion to know precisely what the other partner is really thinking and feeling. The anxiety presupposes that the other partner is being dishonest. More often than not, the other person is not hiding anything other than, perhaps, uncertainty about what he or she feels.

In the early phase of a relationship it helps to practise accepting "not knowing" exactly what the other person feels. It is too soon for either party to know enough about the other to make a prediction about a shared future. Any certainty suggests that one or both partners are staking a lot on imaginary, invented versions of each other.

29

On being possessed

Unfortunately for a woman, a man doesn't understand the simple paradox that to have masterful possession of her, he must surrender to her.

At an impossibly early stage in a sexualised companionship, there intrude feelings of possession – referring to both ownership and craziness. The feelings bring along with them suspicions of betrayal. This is especially so for the partner in the female position.

She deploys her sense of temporary ownership as if it fenced the two of them within an intact enclosure. When a woman asks a man for his commitment to her, she is asking that he enter this intact enclosure for a safe stretch of time during which, with the best will in the world, she will work to secure her possession of the version of him that she wants.

From the man's point of view, or most men's, until they have exchanged marriage vows, even a home-made version of those vows, they are not fenced in, not yet. That day is in the distant future. Until then, he is free. Nor does he embark on researches into her feelings as intent as hers into his.

Given what they really desire, women ask the wrong question when they ask their partner, "Do you love me?" The more accurate question hinges on feelings of being willingly and kindly possessed by the other person. Men, or those who occupy the male position in the relationship, lag behind in their submission to this particular emotional exchange. They feel the need, if at all, only later in the partnership.

Men and women have different notions of possession. If we are trying to find out which partner in the relationship occupies the male position and which the female, one of the determining indicators would be the differing speeds at which they each arrive at the point where they believe they possess or are possessed in the relationship. The moment of shared ownership occurs when they each feel they owe fidelity to the other, when they believe they have seriously and voluntarily committed themselves to a future to be spent cherishing each other, when they happily are each each other's.

A woman will often presume there to be a link between the historical longevity of her devotion and the increased likelihood of a positive outcome to her wish to be had and to have. She supposes that the longer she has suffered from his lack of obligingness towards her, and the longer she has remained constant in her adoration of him, the more likely he is to change in the direction she wants him to, the more likely he is to feel a new gratitude for her patience in waiting for him to finally come round. He will learn, she supposes. Or rather, she supposes that he will learn what she wants him to learn.

She doesn't suppose that he has had plenty of time to confirm that he doesn't want to have her in the sense that she wants to be had. She doesn't suppose that he may hardly think about her. He may well not have noticed that a week has gone by and he hasn't made contact with her, never mind that all this time she has been waiting for him in a particular way, waiting for him to become what she wants him to be.

What does she want him to be? A fiancé, perhaps. Her man, perhaps. The cause of her impregnation, perhaps. Above all, perhaps, someone who lets her know that she completes his being, that he can't live without her, ever, and that he will look after her tenderly so that she will not want to leave him.

In short, she wants him to be someone who validates her reason for existing. After a life-time of being told by the world around her that she is second-rate, even worthless, merely female, why wouldn't this wish become a woman's priority?

Unfortunately, chances are that if he hasn't simply declared his long-term interest, then all this time he's been thinking that they are already having a sort of relationship, even a good relationship. Surely, he thinks, whatever it is that they have, it's enough? Is there anything else to want?

She plods on beside Mr Benighted, hoping that he will realise at last that he can't live without her and henceforth he will look after her tenderly.

Her hope transmutes into assumption. If she waits long enough, he will reward her patience with his love, his faithfulness, his income, preferably all in the form of, yes, here we are again, marriage and children: a good enough reason for being.

Ironically, as we know, the intelligent, independent woman whom we have in mind would be appalled if anyone, especially the man in question, thought that she was "putting pressure" on him and for such embarrassing, unliberated reasons. She would find it excruciating if he had any idea that she thought obsessively about him, that there were times when she could hardly concentrate at work or sleep at night for being preoccupied with thoughts of him. She would be outraged if anyone suggested that her behaviour regarding her new love bears no relation to that of the intelligent, independent woman that she claims to be. She tries to keep it hidden, even from herself, that her infatuation with this man is humiliating and stupid, not least in her own eyes.

The longer she holds out in the face of his intermittent disregard, or his blowing hot and cold, the more certain she becomes, in her well-formed fantasy, of his emotional, sexual, and moral obligation to her. He must reward her with his capitulation. It is her due. Underneath her selfless attendance upon his procrastination, her storm of resentment brews.

Meanwhile, he has not the least suspicion of the tornado of rage heading towards him. He has no concerns about his ethical position because his conduct has been impeccable. He has never promised her a future with him. He loves being with her but truth be told, when he's not with her, he doesn't want to possess her, he certainly doesn't want to be possessed by her. In fact, he doesn't much think about her.

30

Freedom and security

A woman is not secure in a sexual relationship until she can believe that she is in sole, public possession of her partner.

Such an assertion may appall some feminists while others may regard it as an appropriate sense of entitlement.

There is a great abyss between the ideals we aspire to and our capacity to realise them. In distant reaches of the world, there are no doubt communities that contradict this generalisation and we can all cite exceptions in our midst. Nevertheless, scratch the surface of an outwardly wayward or vehemently broad-minded wild woman or libertine and it is likely that even they refuse to share their partner with anyone else. If they indulge in an aberrant, unfettered occasion or interval, it is rarely long-lasting or with amity.

Most people want one person to call their own. The object of the need, once met and seized, is held on to aggressively. Female biology often generates a feeling of urgency to attain that goal as a prelude to establishing a family sanctuary.

Men aren't always in the same hurry unless they want a surrogate mother to mind house for them. Perhaps men's lack of urgency reflects that they have already internalized a feeling of being cared for by one person, and, what's more, that person is usually a woman or someone who can occupy the female position. Perhaps men lack the need to acquire anew either what they already have or what experience has told them spells trouble for them. It is more often the man who feels pressured and coerced into tying the knot.

31
Positive feedback

*P*ositive feedback. Everyone wants as much of it as possible.

Love relationships depend on it for their longevity. Aside from people with very low self-esteem, nobody hangs around negative feedback unless they have been so ground down that they no longer recognize their entitlement to be respected, or unless severe circumstances prevent them from escaping.

Nagging, complaining, critical, angry, self-righteous people who are stingy about giving positive feedback — beware! A partner may leave a partnership in many ways, not all of them literal.

There is a fine line between, on the one hand, unquestioningly enjoying the half-truth of positive feedback and, on the other, suspecting we're being lied to. Nevertheless, we'd rather have positive feedback than not have it. The flattering lies of the well-meaning lover may be incredible but they're far preferable to hearing nothing or hearing the reverse. One part of us knows that the lover is being economical with the truth; the other part refuses to know what mendacity is.

32
Humble pie

If a person's self-esteem is extremely low, someone else's expression of positive regard may not always be able to raise it. The person is unable to believe the complimentary or encouraging remarks directed towards him, can't hold on to the purport of the information, can't hear the nurturing, kind intention.

Being able gratefully to acknowledge a genuine compliment is not merely a question of good manners. It is an indicator of the state of the psyche and, between lovers, of the health of their relationship.

Often the person's negative feelings extend to a self-hatred that gets projected on to others so that either other people seem to confirm the sufferer's worthlessness or other people seem to be worthless too. This destructive vicious cycle underlies racism, prejudice and stereotyping, as well as aggression and violence within and between families. It is difficult to extricate oneself from the cycle. It may require severing a familiar relationship, not least severing a relationship with an aspect of oneself.

When two people's shared psychological boat threatens to keel over during an argument, in a good love relationship one of the partners puts aside his pride and tries to right it. The other partner perceives this as positive feedback, as confirmation that his desirability is greater than his challenger's pride. Showing a genuine wish to make amends, as opposed to going through the motions, is amongst the most useful of impulses because it signals that despite the conflict, the goal is reconciliation.

The relationship is probably beyond repair when one of the partners repeatedly can't allow the other's attempts to make amends, or wants to settle for the appearance of making amends, or secretly has long wanted to end the relationship anyway and is only going through the motions of making amends.

33
Sharing power

All relationships are characterised by a shifting struggle for power, an ongoing dance about who will prevail over whom, who will determine the agenda and what will be excluded from it. Sometimes this fluidity creates difficulties, most of the time it does not, but it always needs to be kept under close observation.

A mature woman who rules the roost at home accepts that when she gets behind the shop counter to serve, it's the customer who is always right. A man who is twisted round the little finger of his young daughter will enter the hospital operating theatre as a senior surgeon and take it for granted that he be treated as a demi-god. Much of our authority depends upon context.

In a healthy emotional relationship, the

dominant position drifts about on the ebb and flow of each partner's emotional moods and needs. The more frequently dominant partner is as likely to be the apron-wearing woman pottering in the kitchen as it is her apron-wearing man pottering in the kitchen. An imbalance of power in a domestic relationship doesn't always show on the surface and only starts to cause problems when the exchange of roles is hampered by resistance.

Andromache and Agrippa

Take the example of the following couple, let's call them Agrippa and Andromache. Early in their relationship, Andromache had an administrative job in a car factory and Agrippa, a construction worker, was trying to develop his own gardening business. Before long he was doing well but the relationship was not.

Andromache could not understand what was happening. After she had attended some counselling sessions and had revisited the chronology of her relationship with Agrippa, she recalled that the beginning of the attenuation of their feelings for each other had coincided with the garden landscaping works on their property.

This is the picture that revealed itself to her. In the first phase of their being together, they had bought a run down old house that had once belonged to a tennis teacher who had built a tennis court over the entire garden. As soon as they moved in, Andromache and Agrippa began playing tennis every day when they got home from work. Andromache, who enjoyed the shared routine, became fit and lithe. In due course Agrippa persuaded her that they should get rid of the tennis court and instead build a beautiful garden that they could both enjoy and use as a showcase for his prospective clients.

He made the garden. Andromache stopped exercising regularly and put on a lot of weight. At home her self-confidence decreased and at work it increased. No surprise, she found herself spending longer hours at the office where she was increasingly well-regarded by her employers. Her status and salary went up. Nearly every night she brought home business tension and more work, distractions from her faltering relationship with Agrippa. As she wryly put it, the relationship became thinner and she became fatter.

Surely, one might ask, working longer hours and earning more and putting on weight provide an insufficient explanation for a disintegrating relationship?

In examining the period of their worsening relations, it seemed to Andromache that something that had been neutral had changed into a sign of Agrippa's dominance. She had been persuaded to agree to the digging up of the ramshackle expanse they had called their tennis court. It seemed to her that she thus had submitted to his wish first to take charge of and then to destroy a precious, joyful, shared part of their lives. That was where the loss showed itself – in their beautiful garden.

There was more than mere figure and fitness at stake. One could accuse Andromache of not summoning an iota of energy to make a separate arrangement for herself, say, simply to go to a gym. What's more, there was a perfectly good one freely available to all the workers at the car factory.

When she stopped to analyse her feelings, she discovered that the transitions in their life-style had paralleled her alienation from Agrippa. It seemed to her that once he had "had" her, his focus of desire moved elsewhere.

It didn't help matters that despite her own success at work, she was jealous of him. She had lost him when they had stopped their jolly volleys across that raggedy net. He had become ambitious to build up his business, an activity that she experienced alternately as making no reference to her or as making full reference to her: he now, she felt, unilaterally occupied a dominant position in relation to her, calling the shots.

It took a while for her to recognise her response as being a big show of rage. She ate a lot, angrily, as if to make herself larger in comparison to him. Agrippa had abandoned her for something that he loved more than her. With him had gone her sense of being in equilibrium with him.

To protect her pride and to mask her hurt, she had abandoned both him and a feminine aspect of herself. She had withdrawn into her work, her stress, her denying body and her dark mood. They had stopped playing happily together. Instead, they were at war.

34
Slow burn

Like the proverbial frog dropped into a pot of lukewarm water slowly increasing in temperature, a person with low self-esteem can become progressively ground down so that he doesn't recognise that he is being treated abusively. The first glimpse of the disaster zone that he's not leaping out of can occur in the middle of a couple's first date or after many years of cohabiting.

Sylvia and Silvius

Take, let's call them, Silvius and Sylvia. Silvius may know that all is not well in their relationship but his psyche is so paralysed that he cannot find the wherewithal to assert himself or shift the power relations or change his circumstances.

Sylvia's attacks on Silvius are small and incremental. They are characterised by subtle, unconscious, passive aggression. She complains about being stuck with him, suggesting a state of scared, domestic catalepsy. She, all the while, draws ample energy to endure her unhappiness by her vigorous use of him as a verbal punch-bag.

Over many years one partner can progressively wreck the other partner's equilibrium with so-called teasing, a sarcastic tone of voice, an angry glance, exasperated sighs, by not passing on incidental pieces of information that need to be shared, by causing small inconveniences by not honouring minor agreements, being unhelpful around the home, contradicting the partner's remarks, withholding sex, and so on. The partner who is being offensive may be aware of blowing the occasional poisoned dart but is probably oblivious of the extent of his or her destructiveness. Meanwhile, the target of the unprovoked attacks may be unaware of its cumulative wearying effect.

Silvius' sneaking suspicion that he deserves ill-treatment increases in proportion to his diminishing self-confidence. The two states nourish each other. His depression or anger or resentment or shame are all unattractive to himself and others, not least his partner, Sylvia. Everyone's reaction to Silvius, their puzzlement or anger on his behalf, confirms for him that he must deserve the treatment that Sylvia metes out to him although he hardly knows consciously how extreme it is.

As he learns, perhaps through therapy, to see its effect upon him, he interrogates himself regarding the hidden gain for him in his having allowed his situation to get to what it is.

Because he feels helpless, he is afraid of not being able to cope if he were to escape the site of his deeply unpleasant circumstances, the relationship. He is paralysed by his anxiety and low self-esteem. If he could budge, where would he go? How would he manage on his own? What would he say to his children and friends and family and work colleagues? He feels guilt. Everyone would think ill of him, would think he was a hopeless case. He thinks of himself as a hopeless case. He feels shame.

The example of Silvia and Silvius shows how the inertia in a relationship is often cemented by the person, in this case Silvius, who ostensibly has less power. He is stuck in a rut and as a result, they are both stuck in a rut, neither confronting nor escaping the possible origins of their unhappiness.

In such instances, attempts to organise a separation are often signs of emotional health returning to one or both partners. The jolt given by the new activity of preparing to go their different ways is sometimes enough to get them out of their rut and start engaging with each other honestly. If they don't actually follow through with divorce, the trigger of seriously considering the possibility of divorce can kick-start attempts to resolve aspects of their earlier mutually destructive power play.

35

The adulterer who loves his wife

While an unhappy spouse may seek solace elsewhere, more commonly a man's extra-marital dalliances have little to do with the pleasure that he and his wife share. They have more to do with the man's psychological make-up, his capacity for empathy, his moral strength, his cultural values, his integrity, his general level of contentment.

There is plenty of evidence that a married man can have sex with someone else without it diminishing the depth of his affection for his wife.

Even disregarding the sex, a married man can fall in love with someone else without it in any way diminishing the love he feels for his wife.

Unfortunately, these facts are of no consequence to his wife.

36
The single woman and the unavailable man

Adultery and possession

A married man who falls in love with a single woman is often bewildered when she wants to end the affair on the grounds that he is married.

He can't comprehend why a single woman who isn't getting it elsewhere should not surrender to the pleasure they can have together in and also out of bed. He'll say, "Let's just relax and have sex and enjoy each other's company." He is saying exactly what single men say.

But he's married. He finds it difficult to understand and may never understand the reason it is more important for her to leave the affair than to endure not having a monopoly on possession of him.

Adultery and guilt

A married man will have difficulty understanding why a single woman ends their relationship because, she says, she feels guilty about betraying his wife.

He can't comprehend why she should feel guilt that more properly belongs to him. After all, he says, his wife has got nothing to do with his mistress, doesn't even know about her.

As philosophers have asked, "If a tree falls in the depths of a forest where no one hears it fall, does it make a sound?"

The adulterous man almost manages to persuade himself that if his wife doesn't find out about his betrayal, he is innocent of it. "It makes no sound," is the answer he would give to the philosopher.

When his wife finds out about his affair, she is deafened by the traumatising news.

Love and possession

A single man with no interest in getting married is bewildered when the single woman he loves wants to end the relationship because he has no interest in getting married.

He can't comprehend why she can't simply surrender to the pleasure they can have together.

"I love you," he'll say. "Let's just relax and have sex and enjoy each other's company," he'll say.

He struggles to understand why it is more important for her to leave the affair than to endure not having public possession of him.

Men and women can have different ideas about love.

37

The other woman and the wife's friends

*W*hat does an abandoned wife think of the Other Woman who stole her husband? Obviously she regards her as the devil's spawn.

The betrayed woman's friend, as a rule, appears to adopt her betrayed friend's opinion. That's what a good comrade should do. She too can't or won't abide the proximity of the Other Woman.

We often see this motif playing itself out when a couple splits up and the man has, or finds, a new partner. Everyone must take sides, supposedly, and the abandoned wife's friends take sides against the Other Woman. Woe betide the friend who does not conform. Managing the display of antagonism becomes painfully complicated when the Other Woman is a member of the same small social community.

Why does a betrayed wife's friend show that she cares so much? To demonstrate to the wife a depth of friendship and loyalty?

The display of friendship and loyalty drives home the gravity of the insult to which the wife has been subjected. Pity for the downtrodden has its barbs. The friend implicitly may assert her self-styled superiority over the wife at the same time as she expresses her sympathy for her plight. Meanwhile, for the wife, being the one who is pitied increases her anger and possible ingratitude towards the friend.

The friends' shared rage against the Other Woman serves also to detract from the group's rage about husbands in general for leaving their wives. It detracts from their rage about men often being financially independent enough to leave a marriage when and where they like.

The friends' rage against the Other Woman masks their shamefaced relief and pride about themselves having escaped being the victim of such humiliation. It masks the ever-present anxiety that the loyal friends' own husbands could follow the first man's example.

38
Covert aggression

Someone's insecurity can be fairly well hidden under the most self-assured surface.

Low self-esteem is a form of self-directed aggression.

A person with low self-esteem may be roused to anger by someone else's supposed high self-esteem, itself merely a mask concealing equally low self-esteem.

Therapy sessions are often concerned with disentangling which elements of your aggression are directed against yourself and which against someone else.

There is the pattern of confessional self-flagellation: "My problem is that I'm a terrible person." Insight will help this become: "My problem is that I think I'm a terrible person."

Or there is the pattern of projection along the lines of: "My problem is that I have to live with the fact that he (or she) is a terrible person." In time this may later become the more useful: "My problem is that he (or she) has a terrible effect upon me and I must either change my response or remove myself from the abusive situation."

Insecurity can disclose itself in small acts of aggression towards the partner. We've all witnessed a couple where one partner does not object when the other is unkind. We're amazed at the oblivion of the put-upon partner who does not complain about being put-upon. There is the "gaslighter" who interjects softly when his wife is speaking vivaciously: "Focus, my dear, focus and keep to the point." There is the unashamed back-seat driver who knows less about driving or directions than the driver does. There is the cruel joker who laughs at someone in order to cause discomfort and if the recipient objects, then insists he was teasing: "Oh lighten up. Can't you take a joke?" There is the person who peppers his mundane observations with a condescending, "You may not know this but —". There is the person who regularly expresses doubt about the veracity of his partner's every factual statement: "Really? Are you sure?" There is the person who can always find a fault in the meal that is painstakingly made for him. There is the person who complains that the partner wants to have sex too often, or not often enough, or that its low erotic rating is the other person's fault.

Bearing in mind that none of this is gender specific, witnesses are amazed at the oblivion of the unkind partner to the transparency of his or her own nastiness. Either he doesn't notice the effect upon his partner although it is staring him in the face every day, or if he does notice, he excuses it by saying something like, "I don't mean to attack her. That's just how I am. I can't help it and if she couldn't handle it, she'd have left me long ago."

Aside from packing one's bags and walking out the door, there are also symbolic ways of leaving. Subtle nastiness may contribute to the quarry trying to escape by means of a displacement activity such as becoming ill or working long hours or drinking hard or developing an obsessive interest in a sport or a hobby or a secret romance, and so on. The unkind person hasn't noticed that the partner has left the relationship.

One sees the insidious effect of subtle aggression in a relationship when the victim of it develops his or her own strategies of equally subtle retaliation, which in turn evokes the other's self-destructive, compensatory responses. Reactions and counter-reactions can become so entwined that the couple end up in a Mexican stand-off where it is impossible to point an accusatory finger at only one of the partners.

39

A masculine obstacle

The tools for the construction of a masculine identity are built into the conventions of every society. Their use is socially condoned or even obligatory.

It's not easy being a man. Sometimes society's usual provisions for the task's achievement are insufficient to undo a man's anxieties about whether or not he can fulfil it. He finds, consciously or not, that he has to take the matter into his own hands. He has to buy a bigger motorbike or drink more than the next man or perhaps just throw his weight around at home and make everyone jump and know who's boss.

Many men associate vulnerability with femininity. Because they are physically stronger than women, some men may attempt to undo the grip of their anxious feelings about their masculinity by displaying a threatening persona or by actually being physically violent.

To deny their terror of their own hidden female aspects, they project their terror into others so that they don't have to contain it themselves. The objects that men attack are often female — or males who are positioned as women for the occasion. This is most vivid in cases of rape, and set-ups analogous to rape, where the victim is overpowered and can hardly fight back, for instance, when a would-be masculine gang attacks a lone individual.

In male-dominated communities, men's fear and denial of their feminine aspects can ratchet up to homicidal and suicidal proportions, for example when a killer kills himself after his lethal attack on helpless bystanders.

A man's difficulty in being at ease with his masculinity, or his supposed lack of it, is a common contributing factor in the disruption of a love relationship.

40

The violent partner

There are different schools of thought around the matter of how to react to a violent partner, bearing in mind that the violence may not always be of the kind that leaves a visible bruise or draws blood.

If your partner hits you once and then is remorseful and promises never to do it again, perhaps he or she should be given another chance. When it happens again, you may be forgiven for wanting to take the kids and leave. If you find that point of view objectionable, then you will surely admit that you are making yourself vulnerable to a third assault. It's up to you.

Almost every child has experienced what feels like abusive treatment from a parent which the parent tells the child is not abusive treatment or, if it makes the child miserable, is for his own good.

Time passes. The child is no longer a child. When adulthood reaches us, unfortunately most of us are in search of a benevolent surrogate parent to make up for the one we lost or never had. We are susceptible to being duped by an authoritarian figure's promises of care, or his or her insistence that what may not feel like care, actually is care, or will soon transmute into care, or will be care in the hereafter, especially if you are obedient.

Meanwhile, there are some damaged individuals who need to dominate others whose interests are the last thing they have at heart. They are probably individuals who were on the receiving end of extremely abusive treatment when they themselves were children.

On the political stage, an egocentric ruler throws just enough meaty bones to the underdog, often in the form of as yet unrealised promises, to make the underdog suppose his subservience is rational and worthwhile. The more that the underdogs can be kept in ignorance, the easier the ruler's control over them. If you have seen the

Greek film *Dogtooth*, for instance, about children deliberately isolated from the world by their parents, you will recognise it as a socio-political allegory of the means by which a single person may exercise domination over others simply by ensuring that they are kept ignorant and thus gullible. This is how the tyrant ensures the underdog's unwitting collusion in his own enslavement.

The political system of South African apartheid, for instance, functioned on this basis with legalised precision. It was the reason that the well-intentioned international cultural boycott of the country at the time was so misguided and cruelly counter-productive: it played straight into the isolationist policies of the apartheid perpetrators, leaving behind it an intellectual and educational desert after the collapse of the old political system . . . its coffers now emptied.

No matter how one wishes to define knowledge, knowledge is power.

We may know our own misery better than anyone else but we are social creatures and need information and communication with the wide world in order to broaden our view and our views, including being able to explore routes of escape from discomfort.

There is a high price to be paid for escaping a violent relationship with a tyrannical partner. This is the reason that so many people — inexplicably, from the viewpoint of outsiders — don't get out even when the prison gate appears to be unlocked.

One of the most difficult psychological tasks before us all is to recognise and then seize our freedom to take charge of our own lives without harming ourselves or others.

It turns out that, after all, it is possible to manage our lives alone, to be good guardians of ourselves, to endure well enough even when we do not possess a surrogate parent. We merely have to let go of the fear that we've borne from childhood into adulthood. This is our childlike fear of the Other, our erroneous idea of an adult, who always seems to be bigger and more grown-up than we are, and dangerous.

41
Breaking up is hard to do

When two people are drawn towards each other for reasons of love or lust or both, each is in his own imagined world. Their goals may only partly overlap. Often each supposes that the other is duty-bound to be the harbinger of fulfilment. Perhaps one partner wants the other to be the prestidigitator of good times right now, while the other partner supposes that a long-term commitment will be pulled out of the hat.

Despite their different expectations of each other, they may well decide to live together. In due course it becomes hard to distinguish between the actor and the acted upon, between who demanded and who volunteered. At last they may reach a point where their firmest concurrence is that they never concur.

Sometimes a break-up is delayed or attenuated: "We'll live apart but still be a couple". They are trying to deal with their alternating guilt and pride, fear and elation. Each person secretly feels that some part of the ending is his or her own fault, secretly feels the despair of profound failure. Publicly they each need confirmation of their blamelessness, reassurance that the failure belongs to the other person.

When relationships break down it's probably impossible, despite later allegations and recriminations, to discover the opening move that began the end. Neither of them can easily let go of the other until the other has admitted to being the originator, the one at fault, the one who owes. This is the reason that contact between them may continue for far longer than logically is necessary.

When there are assets in the picture, the big mistake was not to begin their relationship with a legally formulated description of how these will be arrayed in the event of a break-up. Now everything is in turmoil and they are trying to separate from each other but they tussle over finances. If there are children, they will become pawns on the parents' battlefield.

In the best of circumstances, breaking up is hard to do. Arguments about cash, material possessions and children make it even harder.

Where there are children involved you might argue that the courts are necessary to fix arrangements to do with alimony, custody and access. Even when the supposed primary focus of dispute is the progeny, the law is frequently ineffective against the chemical weapons that divorce uncovers when the children are deployed for covert blackmail in the parents' conflict. When there are no complicating factors such as a parent's addictions or disruptive religious beliefs or unemployment or foreign residence or debauchery, it often happens that after a year or two the arguments about custody and access to the children become less toxic. The mere passing of time effects a depletion of aggressive energy and all-out war fizzles into annoying skirmishes. The acrid atmosphere of battle clears a little and each parent discovers the relief of not only being free of the bonds of a bad relationship but of being released from the pressure of full-time child-care.

42

Breaking up and the law

*W*hen things at last fall apart, usually both partners believe equally that they have been duped, manipulated or exploited in some small or large way. Each blames the other. They may even take each other to court to reformulate their early union of souls as a present separation of assets. They feel compelled to alchemise their angry sense of failure into exultant success.

Recourse to the law allows one or both parties ways of punishing the other for betraying the unregulated, unspoken contract that supposedly bound them in their past cohabitation.

If at all possible, it's usually advisable to use a mediation service and to avoid going to court when divorce becomes inevitable. Bringing in the full force of the law probably means having to dissemble in your description of the relationship, having to engage in a register that bears no relation to the one in which a relationship is conducted. The language has to shift from that of love and loss to that of adversary, from that of emotion to that of economics and logistics. These are modes of communication disconnected from relationship. That said, when the reward for the disjunction is money and revenge, most people seem not to mind the cost of the change of register. They acquire great clarity about their financial worth.

Our society is structured so that men usually earn more than women. In a divorce, the man has more to lose financially than his wife. Curiously, this isn't the main reason that men are reluctant to tie the knot in the first place. There is an awful correspondence between the fact of women usually earning less than men and then women consistently having children without being prepared to be the household's breadwinner if the partnership dissolves. After a break-up, women see themselves as being at the financial mercy of men. Getting money from the man becomes a triumph over his previous supremacy. Women's humiliating subjugation in this post-relationship relationship is so well covered over by societal convention that they usually seem to be oblivious of it.

In many states in America, if not elsewhere, after a one-night stand which leaves her pregnant, for instance, a woman can refuse the man's request that she have an abortion and ensure that he is obliged thenceforth to provide up to sixty per cent of the cost of child support until the child is an adult. Perhaps this law, and others similar to it across the world, is intended to deter men from having pre- or extra-marital sex as well as to support otherwise destitute single women who find themselves pregnant. Unfortunately, it is seized upon equally by women with careers and regular incomes. This raises interesting moral questions about the relationship between women's insistence upon being treated as men's equals and their paradoxically complicit submission to the status of chattel when it suits them financially.

"Child support" from the man whose semen caused the impregnation is essential for the survival of women and children without incomes.

Amongst the middle classes it is a code for the funding of a certain standard of living decided upon by the pregnant woman and supported by the courts.

Unless she lives in a traditional communal setting, the single ethical and independent position that a woman can adopt is to have a child only if she knows she has the means to support the child alone in the event of a separation from the child's father or in the event of his death. Any solution entailing enforced financial support from the child's uninterested or rejecting father is surely neither ethical nor independent. Women's capacity to have children and their drive to have children fixes them in this difficult position.

The best time to involve the legal profession is not when the relationship is falling apart but at its start when living together is going well. This is the moment to compose a legally binding document that itemises the division of the spoil in the event of the relationship breaking up. The loot would include the shared liability for debt, the standard of living expectations, and future child custody arrangements.

Most new couples in love suffer from a

diminution of imagination about worst-case scenarios, an excess of optimism and an increased dose of denial. They perceive early insurance against a non-existent future problem as a squalid, treacherous insult to the intensity of their commitment to each other in the present. But when the love leaves, discussion of money seems to lose its taint.

While statistics vary wildly, about 85% of new relationships eventually break up and of those that don't, 40% end in divorce. Just under half the number of divorced women re-marry and just over half the number of divorced men re-marry. It may or may not be a consolation to women to know that at any one time there are more widows alive than widowers.

A recent survey showed that, at a conservative estimate, 22% of people in a "permanent" relationship have kissed somebody else and 17% have had sexual intercourse with someone else. Another survey revealed that by the end of their lives 60% of married men have been unfaithful with 1.8 lovers, and 45% of married women have been unfaithful with 2.3 lovers.

As for the reluctance to consider the end of a

relationship when it has barely begun, there is only one more inconvenient example of denial in the face of the law. This is when a person doesn't make a will. Making an early will eases the upheaval that ensues later for your partners and heirs. Couples who don't make a will are exhibiting the most extreme instance of denial. Some 40% of liaisons may end in separation but 100% of us die.

43
Having and holding

The partner in the masculine position may not understand that while the detail may vary from woman to woman, his partner, very often or now and then, wants him to make a public display of his affection for her or even merely make a display of their being a couple. All her friends around the restaurant table should hear him order a coffee for her exactly as she likes it; or his arm should be around her when they walk down the street; or there must be a ring on her finger. She wants it known that she has public, quantifiable confirmation that he is hers.

He may appear to the average feminist to be showing her off as his moll, his sex object, his slave, but by these subtle means she is reassured that he, rather, is her slave.

44

Playing house

It can be difficult to pilot safely through the hazardous straits of power relations in a feminist world.

Mopsa and Volumnia

Take for instance the example of a woman, let's call her Mopsa, who is the bread-winner in a fairly new relationship. She sees herself as an independent woman. She complains about her jobless partner's inability to contribute equally to their domestic arrangements, let alone support her financially. She resents his lounging about the house all day, as she supposes, while she's at work. She wants a real man, a man who can earn a proper living and look after her as men, supposedly, are supposed to do.

With difficulty, after too long a time in her view, he finds work. It's not well-paid but it's work. His new employment takes him away from the home every week day.

Mopsa complains that he still needs handouts from her to get through the month. She complains of seeing too little of him because of their incompatible working hours. She complains of his not getting jobs done around the house as a man should do and as he did before he went out to work.

The man can't win.

In a parallel scenario, there is Volumnia. Her partner is self-employed in IT. As long as she has known him, he has always worked from home. Volumnia is a senior school teacher. Her salary is twice his and it is her income that pays most of their bills and the rent on a house that on his own he could never afford.

His working from home means that they can share the child-care. He admits to Volumnia that spending long stretches of time just with their toddler can be irritating, boring and exhausting. When pushed, he also admits that half way through his projects, and he never lacks for employment, he always starts to find his work irritating, boring and exhausting.

While he struggles to find the necessary hours to complete his IT jobs, Volumnia complains that he doesn't do enough housework. He replies that he often genuinely doesn't notice what needs to be done and when he does, can't see that it's urgent. Hers is the usual plaint of the person in the female position. She complains that unless she asks him, he doesn't, for example, do the obvious chores. He doesn't take out the rubbish, empty the dishwasher, help much with their small daughter. He defends himself: he has to meet deadlines and, as she witnesses, he works long hours, conscientiously. He isn't left with the time or the energy to do all she wants him to do or even to be the father to his daughter that he would like to be.

In their sweeter moments together he and Volumnia reassure each other with the recognition that both of them are usually exhausted, overworked, and in his case, underpaid. Unfortunately, most of their moments together have become bitter rather than sweet.

After a few years of playing out a polite conflict

of stereotypes, the marriage is teetering on the edge of an abyss and Volumnia is in therapy. She is worried about the possible collapse of the relationship. She says that they argue all the time and when they aren't arguing she finds her husband increasingly irritating, boring and exhausting.

What are we to make of the two scenarios of the women Mopsa and Volumnia? It is plain that while the emotional factors have a complexity deeper than the complaints that they name, identifying the problem areas is clouded over by a surface issue. This is the women's blindness to how they regard their inappropriate life-styles as a necessary norm. In reality there are two adults in each home but not two huge incomes entering the coffers of each home. They are all living beyond their means and feeling the consequent stress. The women are taking it out on the men who are cast as burdensome children. If they all lived much more modestly, it would matter less that one partner in each case earned relatively little. This sounds like merely the solution a financial advisor would give, but of course it goes beyond that.

Mopsa and Volumnia have locked their partners into a double-bind in which the men can never succeed. In both cases, the woman wants her man to be a commanding, achieving, pro-active presence, an ideal father-figure to themselves, never mind to a child. Simultaneously, the men find that their respective women cast them as juveniles for a reason no more heinous than their relatively low incomes. Both women want their man to be safely under their control, to be the little boy whom mother can reprimand for not helping her enough.

Time passes. Neither Mopsa nor Volumnia gets what she wants. Each man remains as he is, saying that he is doing his best under difficult circumstances but whatsoever he tries, it doesn't please his woman.

It is as if these adults are playing house, trapped in the childlike roles of failed or complaining parent on the one hand and recalcitrant child on the other. As long as this continues the couples will continue to be unhappy, irritated, bored and exhausted.

45
The look of love

Let us set aside, for a moment, important factors such as cultural relativism, narcissism, social pressure, and the psychology of self-esteem.

Most people, if they're being thoroughly honest, will admit that they'd rather a stranger whom they will never see again described them as an unlikeable person than as an ugly person. The same people, without any consciousness of self-contradiction, may also say of a prospective date, "He (or she) should be attracted to me for who I am, not for how I look."

To be rejected for one's appearance, although one's mere surface is being singled out, can feel even more cruelly hurtful than having one's entire being rejected.

Next time you feel awful because you didn't

get near to gaining the object of your desire because, you hate to say, "You weren't the right body-type", reassure yourself by reflecting that your devastated feelings are a Darwinian accident.

Evolution has hard-wired us to prioritise procreation, that is, human survival. During our fertile years and in some cases beyond those, most of us want to be judged as being physically attractive and sexually desirable. We all know that pleasure and contraception aside, the point of sex is babies, and sex starts way back in the arc of events with a mere glance of libidinal attraction exchanged between two people.

Every time you flip through a fashion magazine or glance in the mirror to check how good you're looking, you're connecting to a primitive procreative impulse that you share with a fiddler crab, a hippo and Neanderthal man.

It is curious that human evolution has conjoined sexual rejection and emotional distress. In the competition for a mate, does a male stickleback fish cower in mortification when the female ignores him in favour of his more brightly rouged cousin? It seems not. Is a male tree frog utterly gutted when the decibels of his call can't compete with those of his brother who gets to jump Miss Froggie? It seems not.

In contrast, if you'll forgive the taxonomical leap, human self-regard is at the mercy of the superficial. Unfortunately, it is indisputably true that human aesthetic and erotic preferences in body choice, remarkably constant through time and place, favour the youthful, the comely, the shapely — the god or goddess duplicate who promises reproduction of the type.

Given that we all know this, it is of interest how little effort most of us make to replicate ourselves in the idolized, ideal image that we hold in our mind's eye, the image that gives form to our desire.

There springs to mind the example of the patient, a young woman who was entirely and conventionally beautiful by just about any cultural standards, who decided after much deliberation to attend her friend's forty-fifth birthday party which was to be held at the resort where her friend holidayed every year. While concern about her appearance was never something that the patient worried about, the reason for her hesitating — but not for long — about accepting the invitation was that the venue was a naturist resort.

Later in her sessions she spoke about the impact of the experience. She had been preoccupied by a variety of profound feelings in the course of the event, not least those prompted by her discovery that in the whole crowd of naked revellers she did not see, in her view, a single conventionally beautiful body.

We may conclude that while we can more or less all agree on a norm of conventional beauty, in reality the norm is that most of us are not conventionally beautiful. The norm that is not a norm suggests a paradox that bears thinking about each time you feel unhappy about your appearance.

46
How to spoil a good relationship

Perdita and Pedro

Say for instance someone, let's call her Perdita, has a goal she wants to achieve, a modest goal. Perhaps she merely wants to be accepted by her boss or by her in-laws or she wants to throw a good party where not too much goes wrong or she wants to get through a friend's baby-shower without weeping conspicuously. Perdita simply wants to do something constructive where everything turns out to be ok, for once.

She presumes that she will have the practical assistance of someone close to her, say her boyfriend, a man called Pedro.

It so happens that Pedro, while he means well and agrees to help her, has his own worries. He is only half listening to her mild demands and above all he doesn't share her motivation to achieve her goal. He doesn't appreciate the delicacy of her relationship with her boss; he doesn't see why she can't ignore his parents' obnoxiousness; if she needs help rearranging the room for a party, it can't be helped that he has a bad back; and he certainly doesn't believe that someone else's pregnancy is worth crying over.

In brief, all the signals are flashing at Perdita that she isn't the centre of his world. Pedro may as well be on another planet looking the other way. He's got his own problems at work or with his parents or with his car or his bad back and he doesn't have the energy to focus on her preoccupations. But he always tells her he'll try to do better next time.

At first, wilfully ignoring Pedro's unreliability, Perdita is grateful for his agreement to fulfil her desire and, in this case, help her. She blocks out the signs of his evasiveness. She believes that he owes it to her to give her his full support, that he has an obligation towards her, that he should respond to her reports about her anxieties in her daily calls, texts and emails.

She finds that many of her communications are met with silence and at the eleventh hour, yet again, Pedro is barely available. He doesn't throw himself into the event that is so important to her. She is angry and confused and hurt. He is always present, but somehow not. She finds nothing subtle or subterranean or psychological about it: he always removes himself from her just when or where she needs him most. He repeatedly abandons her. Then he is back – only to let her down again. What can be the reason? She can only assume it is because he doesn't like her and doesn't want her. He is punishing her for not being the person he really wants. Probably what he wants is to end the relationship. It's all over.

The relationship moves into a new phase. Perdita withdraws her tenderness from Pedro, fuming, afraid, depressed, noisy. Perhaps, she thinks, the whole relationship was always a lie. It is all her own fault for being naïve, for not seeing clearly that he was never very keen on her. Perhaps she should re-adjust her ideas about all men. Probably the kind of men she likes, all the men who resemble Pedro, or probably all men, are equally unreliable, rejecting, abandoning and punishing. Perhaps she should have listened to the friends who once warned her off him. Perhaps she should end the relationship and adjust to becoming an old maid. Her anger tempers her depression. How dare he treat her thus?

Meanwhile Pedro is entirely bewildered by her new aggression, her low spirits, her desertion of him. Is it possible that Perdita is frequently abusive, or ignores him and then makes demands, blowing hot and cold, and he has only just started to notice? Perhaps he should have listened to the friends who once warned him off her, or more accurately, warned him off "getting involved" with a woman when he didn't have to.

Their relationship becomes a see-saw of reactions. She assumes that he should be able to read her mind and intuit what she needs him to do for her to keep her happy. Meanwhile, he assumes that they are independent entities and are each responsible for their objectives. What's more, he has never supposed that he should be able to read her mind: how can he know what she wants if she doesn't tell him?

She shouts a lot, in vain, as if to make herself

heard. He becomes withdrawn and deaf to her entreaties.

They have fallen into a plummeting spiral of anxiety and rage driven by projection and supposition. They have both almost talked themselves out of the relationship. But they have only talked to themselves. If they don't soon talk to each other, one, or both, will walk.

47
The child within

When one partner's expectations of the other are rarely met, or when there is insufficient compromise to satisfy both partners' desires, then surviving the disjunction can lead to resentment, insincerity, anger, even despair.

If we were all able to admit to each other early on that we harbour idealised expectations of the other person and then if we were able to lower those expectations to a realistic level, there would be less anger and less hurt in the world. We can't easily do this. We tend to start off a relationship being over-optimistic, wilfully blind to obvious difficulties in the interaction. At the same time we can be brimful of a sense of entitlement. Later we are devastated when our expectations, our fantasies, are not realised. We cease to be able to make a level-headed, unaggressive request of the other person. Destructive impulses well up on both sides.

Because we abrogate responsibility for our own role in our unhappiness, we exaggerate the capacity of the other person to deliver what we want. We pile on the blame and accusation. Meanwhile, the other person is generally equally weak and needy.

In a friendship, you may wonder, "Since I am generous with my attention, honest, fair and kind, how dare she play hard to get? How dare she be manipulative, superior and catty?" If you persist in being disappointed and angry with someone whose amiable attributes were originally of your own invention, it is your own fault for supposing that she is able to be otherwise with you or that she even feels the need to be otherwise. Nor does it mean that you can't work out a way of getting on together again, if that's really what you both want.

Our ongoing infantile narcissism entices us towards an assumption that the world owes it to us to treat us well, or at least, to leave us contented rather than upset. This presumption is evident not only in our personal relationships but in our expectations of our institutions, our financial, military, political and religious establishments. While most of us play no direct part in their functioning, indeed hardly know how they operate, like children we expect to be well served by these parental substitutes. We are outraged when they let us down.

As a rule, we tend not to question our automatic adoption of a child-like role in society. Our first response is rarely to up sticks and leave a bad place or, alternatively, to find out how we can join up with like-minded thinkers to contribute to making our world more agreeable. While we vocalise our noisy protest, send so-called misfits to Coventry, perform media-mediated varieties of bullying as if these were constructive and creative activities, we rarely ask how we can pool our adult skills to participate in learning about and then improving or changing the institutions that we acknowledge we need. It is no surprise that our educational systems are not primarily geared to teach students about how their world works in practical terms. How many of us have passed the modules on how the government operates, or a bank, or the army? How many of us could plumb in a toilet or make a pair of trousers or grow a cabbage? Except for those people who live in subsistence communities and know how to survive, in many ways the rest of us are all infants, incapable of seeing to our most basic needs. Our politicians know that to win a vote they should compete to offer us the biggest handouts rather than require us to participate in managing our own lives, let alone our own communities.

As in the macro, so in the micro. Unless you really are a child or unless you are trapped in a situation of inescapable violence, usually the responsibility for either improving the relationship on the one hand, or simply avoiding it on the other, lies with you.

If it seems to you that resolution of the conflict within you or between you both is not possible, then interrogate yourself. Can you explain to yourself why you choose to remain in the orbit of someone whose proximity makes you very unhappy? Do those reasons justify your not escaping the site of your distress? If it is the defenceless infant within you that forbids your venturing into the adult world, perhaps it will be useful to help that child to grow up before you leave the relationship, and of course, before you blame anyone else for your distress.

Or do you have to leave first in order to be able to grow up?

48

On being too afraid to ask

You can find yourself deeply unhappy because you want something that you are not getting and you are too afraid to ask for it. You are afraid not only of being refused but of the other person's indignation at the topic even having been raised, their indignation that may awake a monster whose attack is your worst fear.

To avoid finding out the truth, that is, the fact of the other's otherness, you refrain from saying what you want. You call your procrastination politeness or "waiting for the right occasion". Really you are hoping that the passage of time, while you neither act nor speak, will magically grant your wishes.

Such procrastination is familiar to us all. It is a familiar distortion of the injunction to be patient.

It is a familiar distortion of the virtue of delayed gratification. It is a familiar distortion of the supposed reward for silence, as if silence will produce action, as if the act of imagining the desired outcome will of itself produce the desired outcome.

In reality, if you do not ask outright, your wish will not be granted, or if it is granted, it will be by accident; or it may be granted as a consequence of your covert manipulation or because it profits the person granting the wish. Then the granting of the wish may turn out to be tainted fulfilment sprung from duplicity, yours or theirs.

But what if you are a person without duplicitous strategies, someone who quietly keeps your wishes and worries to yourself, with no tricks up your sleeve? As long as you continue to suffer at the same time as you can't talk to your partner openly, then all your interpretations of the other's unavailability are mere figments of your imagination.

Quite possibly, when you realise that for a long time your unhappiness has outweighed your happiness, you will find it in yourself to abandon your suffering.

Perhaps you will change yourself in order to be able to speak or, acquiring a new way of thinking and feeling, you will leave the place of your suffering, perhaps even literally leave the relationship.

Sometimes when a person has reached a point where they can make that decision, they have changed so much that they no longer need to leave.

49

Emotional research

Some of the distress that arises in a relationship comes from the despair of knowing one is responsible for having chosen an unsuitable partner in the first place.

You see that you settled on a particular person because of sexual attraction or social pressure or financial security or intellectual excitement. Instead you should have looked for what, in the long run, is all that matters in a close relationship: kindness, care and honesty on both sides.

The period of meeting, attraction and courtship disguise what I call the "emotional research" phase in a relationship. Wrong choices and sad endings are necessary stumbling blocks while we gather information about ourselves and a prospective partner. In the best circumstances, the mistakes and their correction are unpleasant rather than devastating.

You may be keen to team up with someone to whom you're attracted, so keen that you don't pay attention to what you're finding out about the two of you together. You carry on, often feeling unhappy, denying you're unhappy, hoping, with no justification, that the unhappiness will go away. While you stave off the distress of a separation, you prolong your unhappiness in the partnership and dig yourself in deeper. You may look back on your history of break-ups or relationships or non-relationships and say to yourself, "I'm going to do something different this time." The question is always, "Is it really something different or is it the same thing again just dressed up in a different guise?"

We often ignore the warning signals that all is not as it should or could be. We slip into a paralysis of hope that later, somehow, things will change track. Meanwhile, the downward spiral has already been set in motion.

The only solution is to find out how to put on the brakes, stop the rush towards an ending. The way to do this is to find an alternative route that will go in a different direction. For that to happen, you have to both calm down, take a breath, and talk to each other honestly.

50
Conclusion: a good relationship

Before you complain about your partner, consider your reasons and your responsibility for having selected that person in the first place.

You once thought that you chose freely. In some sense, you did.

At the time, the evidence suggests, there must have been some imperfections in the quality or consciousness of, may we call it, your emotional research. The evidence suggests too, of course, that it wasn't all faulty.

Consider the positives, your own satisfied wants and wishes that have kept you in place so far, at your own volition. Then consider the price you have paid for that satisfaction, also at your own volition. Usually the price is the sacrifice of other wants and wishes.

On the scale of pain and pleasure, which is the greater, the cost or the gain?

A good relationship needs a mix on both sides of the following, hard to find, ingredients:

(a) kindness,

(b) honesty,

(c) respect,

(d) loyalty

but most of all –

(e) the choice of a suitable partner to begin with.

Without these five basic components in a relationship, you will find that it's hard to exercise patience, that being forgiving is difficult, and that you have to make greater compromises than you would have to make with a more carefully selected partner.

Unfortunately, none of these sensible suggestions is easily observed, as the contents of this book demonstrate. The overwhelming emotional disruption triggered by infatuation, which we mistake for love, all too often has us more or less lose our reason even as we claim to know what we are doing.

However much you genuinely love your new partner, as long as you stay together you're always going to have to exercise patience, be forgiving, and make great compromises.

Love bites.

Acknowledgements

This book is a slightly revised version of an edition of 2015 published under the title *Love and Sex: fifty therapy lessons*. I am deeply grateful to publishers Adam Rei Books for their faith in the book's revival and their commitment to its rejuvenation.

My sincere thanks go to psychoanalyst Patrick Casement who supervises my clinical practice. It has been the rarest privilege to have had years of access to the professional guidance of someone of his stature. He kindly read a very early draft of this text and made invaluable comments, both critical and encouraging. Of course, any infelicities in this book are entirely my own.

Aside from my ongoing experience with private practice patients, for some twenty years I worked part-time at several National Health Service surgeries in London. I am indebted to those patients for all I learned from them and also to the doctors and staff for providing a consistently benign, thoughtful and supportive environment.

From readers' reviews
of the 2015 edition of this book

"What a privileged insight into the world of psychotherapy! . . . A beautifully succinct précis of the role of love and sex as expressed through therapeutic sessions."

Helen Donlon

"This slim volume punches far above its weight . . . There is something in this remarkable book for everyone."

Jack Klaff

"Highly recommended. This book covers 50 different every-day situations, is a must for all psychology students and graduates who intend working with patients."

Adrian Wolff

". . . A distillation of the therapeutic insights the author has gained from years of treating patients. She shows in a clear and straightforward way how psychotherapy may expose the conflicting feelings the patient has towards his intimate partner so that he may then go on to confront them honestly and deal with them successfully. She also argues that effective therapy lays the foundations for a morality based not only on honesty but also kindness, forgiveness, patience and compromise . . ."

Anon.

From reader's reviews of
Crazy Love: 50 therapy lessons

"I finally feel as if I have some understanding of what psychotherapy is all about and – more importantly – how it might be interesting and even fun. This is a wise, lucid and illuminating account first of precisely what psychotherapy, psychoanalysis and all such therapies are about, followed by some equally wise analyses of what may be going on when you think you've fallen in love. Beautifully written and fun to read and makes psychotherapy sound like an adventure."

Reviewed by "Traveller and Reader"

"Morris' 50 short essays on the questions and issues psychotherapists tackle is a fascinating introduction to her profession. The one danger is that the reader emerges from devouring such compelling topics as 'the adulterer who loves his wife' and 'when good sex is bad news' feeling love is never sane. But Morris offers wise words on what is the secret of a balanced, adult relationship with those we think we love and with society. The challenge is to live up to them."

Reviewed by "Barbara"

Printed in Great Britain
by Amazon

64427209R00121